PRAISE FOR *THE C*
GUIDE TO LIFE AND MONEY

"If building your best life of wealth and prosperity does not include having your own children, Jay Zigmont's *The Childfree Guide to Life and Money* is a must read. Not only does he create a masterful mental framework for childfree wealth creation, but also provides precision when it comes to deploying the necessary tactics. I fully expect this book to become a classic."

—Jordan Grumet, author of *Taking Stock*

"Dr. Jay Zigmont offers what I believe is a first of its kind—financial advice geared specifically to those of us without kids. And it is clear he knows what he is talking about. A childfree person himself, Dr. Zigmont understands what makes our lives unique, how our struggles and dreams aren't so different from others', and how we can best harness our strengths and individuality to plan a life of financial independence and future stability."

—Amy Blackstone, author of *Childfree by Choice: The Movement Redefining Family and Creating a New Age of Independence*

"What a unique and wonderful book! Approximately 20 percent of Americans are either single, have not been able to have children, or have chosen not to have them. But traditional financial planning basically ignores the different needs of this group. As a childfree person myself like Dr. Zigmont and his wife, I didn't need to create an estate to leave to the children, invest in life insurance, or buy a house near good schools. Childfree people aren't following what he refers to as the 'Standard

LifeScript': go to college, get a job, get married, have kids, buy a house, send the kids to college, retire. 'Are we weird?' he asks. If you are an adventurer, a creative artist, or a business owner without children, this book is for you. Filled with stories, statistics, and a unique point of view, this book offers sage financial advice to help you craft a life and financial plan that is uniquely yours!"

—Chellie Campbell, author *The Wealthy Spirit* and *From Worry to Wealthy*

"Everything about the society we live in assumes we'll have kids, and financial planning is no different. Dr. Jay's friendly voice and compassionate, no-nonsense advice—and occasionally, his 'BS detector'—will help childfree and childless folks plan their finances the same way they've planned their families: free from societal expectations about what a good, full life should look like. Whether you want to retire early, live a life you love now, or plan for old age without family support, *The Childfree Guide to Life and Money* is the first of its kind book that will help you get there!"

—Peggy O'Donnell Heffington, author of *Without Children: The Long History of Not Being a Mother*

"Jay's book, much like the man himself, is a real breath of fresh air around life and finances. As a psychotherapist who has been working with the childless-not-by-choice community for over a decade, I was thrilled to see that his book gives as much weight to the beliefs and stories we tell ourselves 'about' money as it does to financial management itself. As well as Jay's paradigm-busting explanation of how the financial industry (and all planning software) is predicated upon the idea that everyone's goal is to leave a big estate for descendants, I deeply appreciated his compassionate inclusion of all types of financial situations, including those in debt and without property or savings. His sections on the different kinds of thinking/planning applicable to 'soloists' (his term) as well as couples and his clear-eyed look at the emotional and financial issues involved in ageing without children (and the pressure to be the default caregivers for parents) are groundbreaking. Although the financial nuts-and-bolts of this book (taxes, insurance, investments, etc) are aimed at a US audience, there is still plenty of useful and fascinating material to make it well worth reading for all of us without children."

—Jody Day, psychotherapist, founder of Gateway Women and author of *Living the Life Unexpected: How to Find Hope, Meaning and a Fulfilling Future Without Children*

THE CHILDFREE GUIDE TO LIFE AND MONEY

MAKE YOUR FINANCES SIMPLE SO YOUR LIFE WITHOUT KIDS CAN BE AMAZING

JAY ZIGMONT

PhD, MBA, CFP®
FOUNDER, CHILDFREE WEALTH®

Cover design by Ploy Siripant
Cover images © Digital Images Studio/Shutterstock
Internal design by Laura Boren/Sourcebooks

Published by Sourcebooks
P.O. Box 4410, Naperville, Illinois 60567-4410
(630) 961-3900
sourcebooks.com

Cataloging-in-Publication Data is on file with the Library of Congress.

Printed and bound in the United States of America.
POD

To my wife, Vicki, who will always be my Rose.

CONTENTS

INTRODUCTION

If you are Childfree or Permanently Childless, this book is for you. Your life and finances shift when you don't have kids and aren't planning on having kids. It does not matter if it was by choice or not by choice. **Your reason for not having children is yours alone.**

In its simplest form, some people connect being Childfree with those who choose not to have kids and being Childless with those who didn't choose this life. Unfortunately, this dichotomy is overly simplistic. In reality, there is a continuum of terms and beliefs around children, ranging from those who are Childless Not By Choice (CNBC) to those who are antinatalists. From my perspective, where you are on the continuum has minimal impact on your financial plan.

I am going to use the term "Childfree" throughout this book. While there is still considerable debate about which word to use for nonparents, I choose Childfree because that is the term my wife and I use. But feel free to substitute whatever term you prefer. The term isn't what matters. What matters is the impact that comes from not having kids.

When you are Childfree, you have thrown out the "Standard LifeScript" and are in somewhat uncharted territory. There is more about the LifeScript in chapter 2, but this is the societal notion that you need to go to school, get married, buy a house, have kids, retire, pass on your wealth, and so on. The LifeScript is built into our culture, religion, taxes, finances, government, and more. Deviating from the LifeScript can cause you difficulty in relationships, but it also allows you to make completely different choices with your life. **Living a life of Childfree Wealth® means you have the time, money, and freedom to do what you want.**

Being Childfree does not automatically make you rich; income disparities still exist. The difference is that Childfree people can follow their passions, even if those passions do not lead to giant net-worth figures. If we want to open a cupcake shop, which isn't that profitable, we can. If we want to travel the world or be a nomad, we can. But beware that being Childfree may mean so much flexibility that we get stuck in analysis paralysis from having too many choices.

With flexibility and choices in mind, this book starts by helping to outline what it is like to live a Childfree life and how to make the most of it. While many other financial books may start with finances so you can retire and enjoy your life, being Childfree flips that. Being Childfree means that you can live the Financial Independence, Live Early (FILE) lifestyle that focuses on the right work at the right time and that means something to you. It means more options earlier in life, including taking a sabbatical, embracing the Gardener and the Rose system (which I'll explain on page 59), and even challenging bedrock ideas like needing to buy a house.

The book's second half dives into how being Childfree changes your finances and how to reach your goals. It starts at the end of your life, with a realization that if you don't care about passing money on to the next generation, your entire financial plan changes (much akin to the concepts from the book *Die With Zero* by Bill Perkins). I dive deep into common financial and life fears, including the BINGO question: "Who will take care of you when you are older?" **I aim to keep your finances and financial plan simple, so your life can be extraordinary.**

A note about privilege and understanding where you are: I acknowledge my own privilege and the fact that everyone struggles with money differently. I grew up broke, but I was able to learn about finances and succeed financially. It was a rough road for me at times, and it is even harder for other people. I outline here a process to take control of your own finances and make them fit your life when kids aren't part of the picture. Where you start will likely impact where you end and if you are able to live and give generously. The key is to keep your focus on the improvements you have made and not on where you may be falling short. I freely admit that my personal financial plan is not perfect, and I've made more than my fair share of mistakes. We all need to have grace for both ourselves and others, in addition to acknowledging our own privilege throughout this journey.

HOW TO USE THIS BOOK

While you are welcome to read the book cover to cover, you may get more out of it by using each chapter as a reflection tool to help create your own life and financial plan. If you use the book as a framework, you will first identify the life you want to live, then create a financial plan to get there, and finally, make sure you don't pay more taxes than you have to.

This book is a bit of a "choose your own adventure" book. Since Childfree people do not all follow the same script, it was nearly impossible for me to outline a linear path for everyone. There will be chapters that fit you and ones that don't. Skip the ones that do not apply right now. You may come back to them later, and that is okay.

Throughout the book, you will find links to courses in the Childfree

Wealth® Academy, labeled "Diving Deeper." Childfree Wealth® is my company, and it is a life and financial planning firm dedicated to serving Childfree people. The academy includes courses, videos, references, and group Q&A sessions (via Zoom). You will need to sign up for the system first before you can use the links in each chapter. Access to the academy is normally $50 per month, but since you bought this book, you get one month free with coupon code 30DAYS. Go to https://childfreewealth.com/academy to sign up. If you are overwhelmed, that is normal and we are happy to help. We offer a Childfree Wealth® check up that does a deep dive into your life and finances. Think of it like getting a routine physical, it identifies what is going well and any areas that are concerns. You get to meet with a Childfree Wealth Specialist® and get a professional opinion, which can help you to prioritize and know about any big concerns. To learn more, visit https://childfreewealth.com/schedule-meeting.

PART I:

CREATE THE LIFE YOU WANT

1
ARE WE WEIRD?

Are you happy with your life?

"Very. I love my husband, and I love the life we've created. I wish I could show childhood me what I'm up to because I think she would be proud and think I am a badass. I also think she would be relieved. I think she would see that while I am married (like she always expected), I don't have kids, and my life is full of fun, joy, and adventure (which she didn't expect). She would be relieved that I am healthy and happy and not a mindless drone who did what all her high school friends did. She would be proud she escaped the narrative she had been force-fed her entire life."

—CECILIA, TWENTY-FIVE, MARRIED

When I set out to look at the impact of being Childfree on life, wealth, and finances, it started with a simple question: "Are we weird?" We, in this case, means my wife and me. Now, I will admit that we are probably weird in many ways. After all, we both have PhDs, and our date nights regularly include designing research studies, but is our life without kids "weird"? Is it weird that we don't care about how much money we pass on? Is it weird that we moved 1,200 miles on a whim for a better job? Is it weird that we can do whatever we want and not worry about anything but taking care of our two mastiffs (and jerk cat)?

SPOILER ALERT: We may be weird in comparison to those with children, but next to other Childfree people, we are remarkably normal.

Part of the reason why we wondered if we were weird was that everyone else around us had kids or were having kids at the time. While kids were not a choice for us (my wife has a 50/50 chance of dying if she gets pregnant, which made our choice to be Childfree relatively straightforward), the pressure was still there. We were happy with our life, but many others were unhappy with our choice. Here's an example: One day I was at work when one of my staff members stopped me in the hall and said, "I've been thinking about you and your wife. You are both smart and you really should have kids..." We can have a separate discussion about whether this is an appropriate thing to discuss at work with your boss, but the bottom line is that my employee was putting her own judgments on us. She had three kids and that worked for her, just as it works for us to have no kids.

Most Childfree people have their own stories of being judged. When you do not match the "norm," people seem to feel comfortable judging you. Or worse, they ignore your life choice and assume you will change your mind. For some people, it is a choice not to have kids; yet for others, it is not. Either way, it is easy to feel like an outlier or not fit in when you are Childfree or Permanently Childless.

Like many others, at first, I didn't even know that my wife and I were Childfree or that there was a term for it. I first saw the word "Childfree" on Reddit when I started reading r/childfree. The r/childfree community let me know that others are out there (they have 1.5 million members). At least I now knew there was a term for us.

At about the same time, I started working on the education process to become a CERTIFIED FINANCIAL PLANNER™. The interesting thing to me was that while the financial literature talks about not having kids yet, or having an empty nest once the kids leave the house, it never once mentions what to do if people are never going to have kids. When you look at the research, such as the 2022 study from Michigan State University that found that 1 in 5 adults self-reported to be Childfree, it is incredible that 20%+ of the Unites States is wholly overlooked in finance.[1]

JUST HOW COMMON IS BEING CHILDFREE?

Being a researcher, I had to dive deeper. I set out to read everything I could get my hands on and to talk to as many people as possible. In the end, 299 Childfree people responded to my survey, and I interviewed 26 (all in the United States). This research was the foundation for this book and my first, *Portraits of Childfree Wealth*, along with the framework for my life and financial planning firm, Childfree Wealth®.

> WARNING: I will nerd out on data for a bit here. I won't be offended if you aren't a data nerd and want to skip to the next section.

1 Zachary P. Neal and Jennifer Watling Neal, "Prevalence, Age of Decision, and Interpersonal Warmth Judgements of Childfree Adults," *Scientific Reports* 12 (2022): https://doi.org/10.1038/s41598-022-15728-z.

The first question I wanted to understand was: How many of us are out there? My initial research found a 2018 study from the U.S. Census that looks at Childless adults over fifty-five.[2] After a deep dive into those numbers, I estimated that 11% of those aged fifty-five and over in the United States are Childfree (defined as don't have kids and don't plan on having kids). A few years later, the Michigan State study found that 21.6% of respondents identified themselves as Childfree. The Michigan study was a survey of people only in Michigan but had a much younger population. The bottom line is that there are a lot of Childfree people out there, and the percentage is growing among younger generations.

The second question was about regret and happiness. It is common to hear from others that when we reach old age, we will regret being Childfree. It is possible I might regret being Childfree, but it is also possible that I might regret not being an astronaut (and neither is a choice for me). What did the data say? At the end of 2021, I did my own dive into how being Childfree impacts life and finances. I did a survey that had 299 respondents and interviewed 25 of those who completed the survey. As part of my survey, I asked, "Are you happy with your life?" The overwhelming answer was yes (281 people replied this way, or 94%). Respondents shared that they were happy with their life overall, and particularly their freedom. Even those who said they were unhappy were quick to say that it was not because of being Childfree but because of other issues in their life.

So there are a lot of us, and we're happy. Not a bad start. But why do people choose to be Childfree? It is not surprising to me, but it may be to some that Childfree people put a lot of thought

2 Tayelor Valerio, Brian Knop, Rose M. Kreider, and Wan He, *Childless Older Americans: 2018,* Census.gov, August 2021, https://www.census.gov/content/dam/Census/library/publications/2021/demo/p70-173.pdf.

into their choice. In fact, 53.17% of participants had more than one reason. Here is an overview of the major reasons people choose to be Childfree:

REASON FOR NOT WANTING CHILDREN

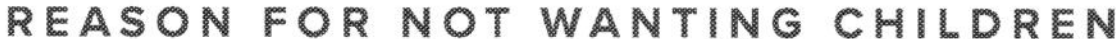

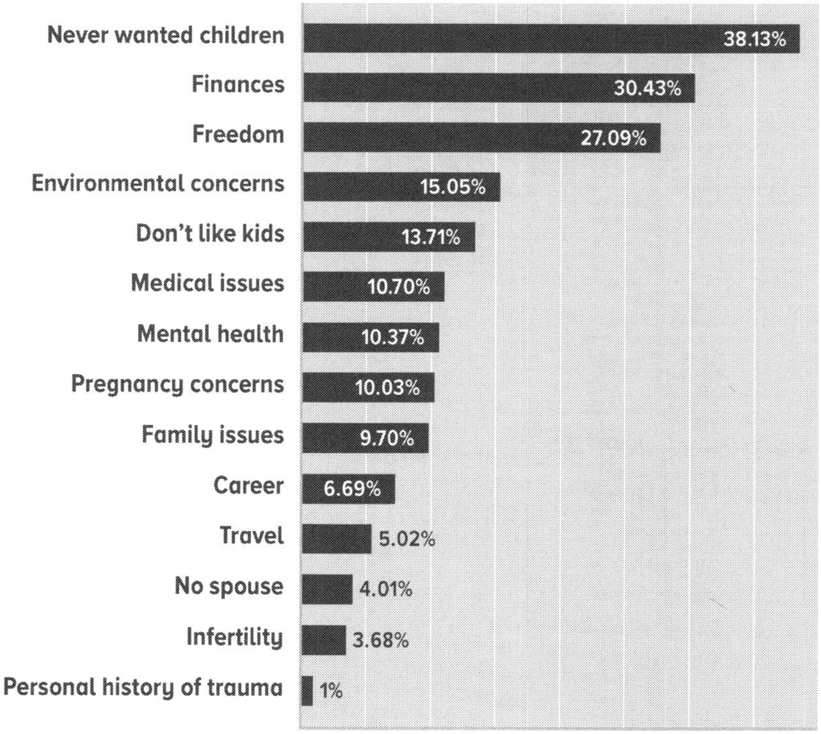

While each person had their own reason for being Childfree, the one commonality with most of the answers has to be the amount of thought and depth that people put into their choice:

> "I don't want to deal with the emotional, financial, and physical toll that children take. On top of that, I'm essentially infertile, making the financial aspect of having kids even greater. I see my coworkers and family dealing with life with kids and the emergencies and surprises that come along, and I'm glad I don't have to deal with that every day."

In hindsight, my study was skewed toward Childfree people rather than those who are Permanently Childless. Some of the reasons stated may not be by choice (medical, family, spouses or lack thereof). The bottom line is still the same: The choice (or not by choice) to not have children is complex for most.

ARE CHILDFREE FOLKS BETTER OFF FINANCIALLY?

The census report[3] found that among adults over fifty-five in the United States, Childless single women had the highest net worth ($173,800), but it wasn't statistically significant. Here are some high-level numbers from my research:

Income: The median income range for Childfree people was $60,000–$89,999 in the study. In comparison, the overall U.S. median income was $54,132 for the same time period for adults.

3 Tayelor Valerio, et al., *Childless Older Americans: 2018.*

Debt: The overall percentage of Childfree people carrying any type of debt was similar to that of the U.S. population overall. For example, 55% of Americans carry a balance on their credit card, compared to 53.18% of Childfree people.

Assets: Assets represent everything you own. Overall, there wasn't much difference, but while 65.5% of those in the United States own a home, in comparison, 55.18% of the Childfree survey respondents own a home.

Net Worth: Your net worth is everything you own minus everything you owe. Rather than look at the median or mean net worth, it was helpful to look at categories of net worth. Interestingly, while approximately 9% of the United States are millionaires, 13.4% of those Childfree people surveyed are millionaires. At the same time, an Aspen Institute study found that 11% of the United States have a negative net worth, while in the Childfree sample, it is 32.4%.[4]

There is room for a lot more research based on the financial numbers, but the bottom line is that being Childfree does not protect people from income and wealth disparities.

THE RULES DO NOT APPLY

In the end, my wife and I are "normal" within the sample of Childfree people but far outliers in the general population. This may be true for

4 This could be a result of net worth measures. If Childfree people are embracing a *Die with Zero* approach, they are not holding on to their wealth, which would lead to a lower or negative net worth number. My experience with clients backs this up, but more research is needed.

you and many others. Since we are such outliers, general rules, especially in finance, are not likely to fit. For example, the general rule is that you need ten to twelve times your income in life insurance. The key is that life insurance should be there to protect your income after you pass, but only if someone is relying on your income. If you are Childfree and single, there is almost no need for life insurance. If you are in a couple and both of you are working, chances are you don't need life insurance either.

The challenge, then, is to stop comparing yourself to others and craft a life and financial plan that are uniquely yours. In finance, we love benchmarks, or measures, to know if we are doing "good" or "bad." Most benchmarks assume you do have children (or will have them), so they are not valid comparisons. I've found that many Childfree people do not really want to retire, so even measures about how much money you should have to retire may not fit. Retirement is an option for Childfree people, not a requirement. Rather than following the classic path of working twenty-five years and getting the "watch," Childfree people tend to focus on doing what they enjoy and cutting back over time. Even comparisons within the Childfree community may not be helpful, as the amount of flexibility we have means we all live vastly different lives.

The question to you is, what do *you* want to do with your time, money, and freedom?

DIVING DEEPER: For more, visit https://childfreewealth.com/104.

BUCKING THE STANDARD LIFESCRIPT

Throughout this book, I will mention the "standard life plan," or "Standard LifeScript," and talk about how the lives of Childfree people may be different. The Standard LifeScript is the one that society, family, culture, and religion preach. It includes the following steps:

1. Go to school (and get good grades).
2. Go to college.
3. Get a job.
4. Get married.
5. Buy a house.
6. Have kids.
7. Send your kids to college.
8. Retire.
9. Pass on wealth to the next generation.

This plan is so ingrained in our culture that many adults play it out without even realizing. They may "wake up" later in their life and ask how they got there. In many cases, the Standard LifeScript becomes a bedrock assumption for financial planning.

The problem with the Standard LifeScript is that if you deviate from it, you no longer "fit" as part of the norm. While I don't know if it was ever my goal to be "normal," it can be challenging to be different. There is pressure from family and friends, culture, religion, and more to conform to the norm.

Here's an example. My wife and I started with the Standard LifeScript. We went to school, got jobs, and planned to get married. My wife was raised Catholic, and I was raised Methodist. Her family wanted us to get married in a Catholic church, which I was okay with. We met with the priest to start the process but quickly hit a snag. It turns out that to get married in a Catholic church (at the time), you had to not only agree to raise your kids Catholic but also agree TO HAVE kids, which wasn't an option for us. It did not matter that my wife was an altar server in that church. The two other Catholic churches we tried had the same answer. Ultimately, we weren't conforming to the norm, so we had to change our wedding plans and get married in the Methodist church. We have been happily married for fourteen years, so it worked out, but it was quite an eye-opener.

It is not only religion where the life plan is ingrained. A quick review of the tax system shows that the federal government actively supports the standard plan (marriage, kids, home ownership, etc.) and ignores single people, Childfree folks, and renters. In states that have laws against discrimination based on familial status, they only protect people with kids. They do not protect people without kids. Employer benefits support having kids (maternity and paternity leave, adoption benefits, day care, etc.), and most cover only legally married couples, not long-term unmarried partners.

We all need to be aware of the Standard LifeScript, as it often forms our core mental model or belief system of how life is "supposed" to happen. The hard part with mental models is that, for the most part, they are tacit or unconscious beliefs that we compare ourselves and others to. Even when we consciously decide to live a different life, we may find ourselves drawn back to the norm due to the power of the Standard LifeScript. The key is to be aware of our decisions and whether they are part of our own life plan or if we are just being drawn back to what's expected of us.

A powerful way to cope when you are being drawn back to the

Standard LifeScript is to ask yourself: *Whose voice is telling me I need to do this?* You will find that, in many cases, it is not your voice but that of your parents, culture, religion, or society. For example, buying a house is a choice for Childfree and Childless people, not a requirement. Even though buying a house is not actually a requirement for anyone—Childfree or not—I regularly hear from people who say that they must buy a house because it is the "right" thing to do. This is all head trash from the Standard LifeScript that may or may not fit your own life and financial plan. (There is more information about buying a house—or not—in chapter 18.)

A SPECIAL NOTE FOR PEOPLE WHO ARE CHILDLESS NOT BY CHOICE (CNBC):

While much of this book fits Childfree and Permanently Childless people equally, people who are Childless Not By Choice (CNBC) have some unique concerns regarding shifting from the Standard LifeScript to their own life plan. When you are CNBC, there is typically a need to grieve the life you thought you were going to live before you can start to envision a different life and future. If you have not made it through the grieving process yet, or are still trying to conceive, you may want to put this book down until later. It is hard to envision a new life plan when you are not ready.

If you are Childless and still trying to work through the process, I encourage you to find a community and people who can help you through this process. I have had the pleasure of working with Katy Seppi from Chasing Creation, and she has taught me a lot about what it means to be Childless. Her community is only for Childless women and non-binary people and is a supportive environment where you can grow and make your way through the grieving process.

DIVING DEEPER: For more, visit https://childfreewealth.com/cvc.

Other ways Childfree folks don't fit the norm

U.S. Census data says that 32.1% of Childless adults over fifty-five were never married (as compared to 2.5% of parents). As I've dived deeper into the data and worked with Childfree people, I have found a wide range of family structures in our community, and marriage is just one option. Some people are single for life, others in long-term committed relationships, in groups (romantic or not), and in as many combinations as possible. The Standard LifeScript says marriage is the only option, so it is yet another area where we don't fit the norm.

From a financial standpoint, many Childfree people don't really want to retire, and most don't care about how much money they have when they die (as long as they don't run out). The days of working twenty-five years to get the proverbial gold watch and pension are gone.

Most do not aim for intergenerational wealth, and adding more zeros to the bank account can seem pointless.

The bottom line is that for many of us, we may follow very little or none of the Standard LifeScript, even though society says it is the only way. Building awareness of how you fit or don't may help you figure out your own life plan and what matters to you.

DIVING DEEPER: For more, visit https://childfreewealth.com/lifeplan.

2

CHOOSING A LIFE PLAN THAT IS YOURS

Why did you decide to be Childfree?

"When I was young, I suffered from depression and a very low baseline of energy. By my early twenties, I found adult life a struggle and realized that I would not have the energy or emotional bandwidth to care for a child AND work full time. I also suffer from chronic pelvic pain and did not want to exacerbate it with pregnancy and childbirth. Later in my early thirties, I developed a migraine disorder that would make daily life fifty times harder than I ever thought it would be... I want to use my free time to relax, manage my chronic pain symptoms, do whatever I want whenever I want, save for retirement, and spend time on creative pursuits. I don't see a possible reality where I would be happy about raising a child."

—DIANA, THIRTY-THREE, LONG-TERM RELATIONSHIP

FIGURING OUT WHAT'S NEXT

As part of my research, I asked "What does it mean to live a life of Childfree Wealth?" While there were a wide variety of answers, in the end, living a life of Childfree Wealth means that you have the time, money, and freedom to do what you want. It does not mean you are automatically rich or automatically anything, but the options are endless when it comes to deciding how to live your life.

The challenge is that there may almost be too many options if you throw out the standard life plan. What happens for many Childfree people, myself included, is that they try to stick to the Standard LifeScript for as long as they can, but then they hit the Childfree Midlife Crisis (more on that in the next chapter). The realization then is that there is no more script to follow, and now you are on your own.

If you are reading this and freaking out about running out of what you are supposed to do, that is okay. I will take you through a menu list of options for things to put into your own unique life plan. There is no way I can cover every option, but there are common questions that Childfree people often ask themselves, and that is an excellent place to start. But first, be aware of analysis paralysis.

When thinking about what you want to do with your life, you can easily get stuck in analysis paralysis or suffer the paradox of choice. Analysis paralysis happens when we overthink a problem and don't take action. It is similar to the paradox of choice in that having too many options may actually cause people not to choose at all. If you have never gotten stuck in analysis paralysis, consider yourself lucky. Many people can get stuck overthinking things and trying to get them "right" the first time. There are books dedicated to helping people work through analysis paralysis and overthinking, so I won't address everything here.

I can say it is okay to try something, decide it wasn't the right choice, and then try something else. This goes for all areas of your life. Take a chance and try new things. Set initial goals and dreams in your life plan; it is okay if they morph over time. There are very few choices in the life of Childfree people that can't be undone or changed. Take your best shot at a plan that is yours, and you will learn more about yourself and what you truly enjoy as you execute that plan.

The key is to be aware when you are stuck in analysis paralysis. You can try giving yourself a timeline to decide, and then you must act. I allow myself one day to be stuck in my head on anything. While working on my PhD dissertation, I found that after I got feedback from my advisor, it would take me a month or more to beat myself up before I could make progress. If I kept beating myself up for months, I would never get my dissertation done (or this book, for that matter). After I noticed this habit, I switched to giving myself one day for a pity party and finished my dissertation in record time.

Here is another silly example that may help you to see when you are stuck. My wife and I have different tactics when choosing a show to watch. My wife loves to watch the "click, click, click" channel (i.e., when you are looking through every streaming app for just the right show or movie). She will regularly spend fifteen to thirty minutes clicking, to end up with us just watching *The Bachelor* again, which is her go-to. On the other hand, I will pick one streaming app, look at the recommendations, and pick something that seems marginally good. Sometimes it works out for me, and sometimes it doesn't. It is okay when it doesn't work out, as there is always something else to watch, and sometimes I'm pleasantly surprised with what I've selected.

The key is to pick something, and if you do have to look at everything first, just set boundaries around how much thinking you will do. Life can pass by quickly while you are just clicking mindlessly.

What do you want to be when you grow up?

The core question of your life plan is simple: What do you want to be when you grow up? I ask this question of all my clients, from those in their twenties to their eighties. It has nothing to do with age but reflects moving to another stage in your life. It may reflect choosing a different career, dedicating yourself to service, or just enjoying your time on this Earth. It is different for each person, but it is the overarching, existential question we all feel compelled to answer at some point.

The challenge is that you need a direction in your life or your financial plan, and the rest will not matter. In my interviews for *Portraits of Childfree Wealth,* I regularly heard it explained as identifying the impact you want to make on this world. *Impact* is a big word, and everyone I interviewed took a different approach.

Let's take Jesse, for example. He and his wife live in an RV in Colorado with their two cats. She works in healthcare, and he is working on creating a video game. In the video game world, either your game takes off and you get rich, or you make very little. He is aware of that dichotomy but sees his game as a way to make an impact. I got to play a demo of his game, and it is an open-ended game that mirrors life with effectively infinite choices, and the player gets to choose their own goals. Jesse has decided to make a game that may help people be mindful of their own life choices. He explained that he might not be able to measure the impact of his game or his other writings, but he hopes that he can impact people's lives and help them to make better life choices. Jesse has shifted his entire life to create a more significant impact. Living in an RV may not be for everyone, but it allows them to control costs, and he can focus on his passion.

You need to decide what impact you want to make and the life you want to live. For Stephen Covey fans, this is habit number two: "Begin with the end in mind," from *The 7 Habits of Highly Effective People.* It may also be your legacy. It will be what you do when you grow up (even if you never *really* want to).

Three questions for life planning

George Kinder, founder of the Life Planning movement, developed a set of three questions for life planning that may help you figure out what you want to do. I use them frequently with clients, often with surprising results. If you are in a couple, review the questions individually first, and then share them with your partner. Your best bet is to journal your answer to each question thoroughly before moving on to the next one.

1. I want you to imagine that you are financially secure and have enough money to take care of your needs, now and in the future. The question is: How would you live your life? Would you change anything? Let yourself go. Don't hold back your dreams. Describe a life that is rich and completely yours.
2. Imagine you visit the doctor who tells you that you have only five to ten years left to live. You will remain as healthy as you are today and won't feel sick, but your time is restricted. What will you do in the time you have left?
3. Finally, imagine your doctor says you have one day left to live. Notice what feelings arise as you confront your very imminent mortality. Ask yourself: *What did I miss? Who did I not get to be? What did I not get to do?*

Given the answers to the questions above, I want you to ask yourself one last set of questions:

What do I need to change now?
What do I want my life to look like?
What would the future me wish I had done?

Before you go any further, I want you to engage your bullshit detector. If you were sitting across from me right now, I would be looking for areas where you are BSing yourself (and me). Look for areas where your answers to Kinder's questions do not match what actions you think you need to take.

Here's an example. I met someone who, in their heart, always wanted to be a librarian. If she had all the money in the world, she would be a librarian for free (Kinder's first question). If she had five to ten years to live, she would quit her job and return to school to work on her master's in library science (Kinder's second question). She had no regrets in life (Kinder's third question). When I asked her what she needed to do based on those answers, she told me, "I should be saving more money." I asked why, and she recited a list of things you are "supposed to do" (Standard LifeScript), and she knew she was behind in saving money. In reality, she was doing fine financially, and what she needed to do was enroll in that master's program in the fall, which, by the way, her current employer would pay for.

The challenge with life planning is that it causes conflicts between the Standard LifeScript and the one you want for yourself. When you are Childfree or Permanently Childless, you need a new life plan, as the standard one won't fit, no matter how hard you try. Your life plan must reflect your wants, needs, and wishes—not anyone else's. If you live your life on someone else's plan, you might just hit someone else's goals and not be happy.

Want an example of how things can go sideways if you follow a plan that isn't yours? In my previous career, I was in healthcare and did a lot of work with aspiring physicians. I often met with struggling medical residents and coached them on life and learning. I met one resident when he was in his last year of medical residency. For those who don't know, physicians do three years (or more) of residency after completing their medical degree. This resident was doing okay, but not great, and struggled at times. After meeting with him for a while, it came out that he never really wanted to be a doctor. His heart was in art. His family (and culture) said he had to be a doctor. His family paid his way through medical school. He was profoundly unhappy. After soul searching, he decided to leave medicine and go into art. I saw him a year later, and even though he was making very little money and his family was furious, he told me he had never been happier. I give him a lot of credit, as very few people could make such a dramatic change for their happiness, and I'm proud of him.

What brings you joy in life?

The bottom line is that you need to Marie Kondo your life: focus on what brings you joy, and throw out the rest. All too many people get stuck in jobs because they have great benefits or a great salary. If you are staying at a job you don't like for the money or benefits, you have just identified the minimum you have to be paid to be unhappy. If you are living somewhere you don't like, maybe it is time to move. If you are unhappy with the people around you, it may be time for a change.

Across the rest of the book, I will work hard to knock down the barriers that are keeping you from joy in your life. Before diving in further, identify your true north and where you want to aim. It may change over time, but this book is about enabling you to chase your goals and dreams, not the ones we all feel like we are required to chase.

DIVING DEEPER: For more, visit https://childfreewealth.com/105.

THE CHILDFREE MIDLIFE CRISIS

Having a life plan may not prevent you from hitting the Childfree Midlife Crisis, but it may help you to get through it. I define the Childfree Midlife Crisis as the moment when you hit your personal, professional, and financial goals and then go, "Now what?!?!" The crisis does not have to occur at a certain age, but it often comes when you realize you have done as much of the Standard LifeScript as you want to and now have run out.

Childfree people experience a different midlife crisis than parents. When parents hit their personal goals, they often shift their time and effort to their kids' goals. We could dive deeper into whether they are really their kid's goals or just projections of the parents, but that is not for me to judge. The difference with Childfree people is that once we hit our goals, we cannot easily shift them to the next generation. We also tend to have different long-term goals, as Childfree people tend not to prioritize passing on generational wealth, which means that just adding more money to our bank account doesn't help.

I hit the Childfree Midlife Crisis hard at about age thirty-eight. I had achieved my personal, professional, and financial goals and was burned out from my work in healthcare. Before burning out, I had been a paramedic, and then I moved into healthcare education and eventually became a healthcare executive. While I focused on treating patients and saving lives, I ultimately realized that healthcare is really about finance, even in nonprofit organizations. I was at a loss for what to do next.

My wife and I take turns between who is growing and who is providing support. We decided she would hit the job market, and we would move to wherever she got a faculty position. I put my time and energy into helping her, partially so that I didn't have to address my own crisis. I would go on to run a business selling items on eBay and Amazon and running a maple syrup farm. Neither of these used my skills, but they kept me busy. I made some money selling online and lost some in farming, but I was still lost in a greater sense of the word.

When I turned forty, I started reflecting on my future, and then I was walloped when one of my friends from high school passed away. I hadn't seen her in years, but she was the first of my peer group growing up to pass. It took me a while to process, but it was a wake-up call. I realized that I needed to find a new path and plan and appreciate the limited time we have in life. I still needed to support my wife, but I also needed a plan for myself.

I realized that my skills are in helping others to learn, grow, and achieve their goals. I could take my experience in coaching and my PhD in adult learning and put them to use helping others. My impact could improve lives, and I could make some money simultaneously.

I share my story not because it is easy or because I like telling it but because I want to show that we all struggle. In five or so years, I was lost, we moved three times, I went back to school to get my CFP® certification and MBA, and I started my own company, Childfree Wealth®. I'm not going to say I have it all figured out, but at least I am now aware of what matters—and what doesn't—in my life and my life plan.

Hitting a breaking point

The first thing you need to do is be aware that the Childfree Midlife Crisis exists. All too often, I will meet people who are having trouble sleeping, feel like they are in a funk, and are stressed or burned out. As I pull apart what is going on, they are often at the crisis point or at a crossroads between the Standard LifeScript and what they want to do with their life.

I met someone recently who needs to quit her job. Even though her job pays well and has allowed her to support her husband in his growth, she has put herself aside for her entire life. She has a passion for writing and making an impact with her writing. She and her husband are DINKS (dual income, no kids) and could live on either salary. I encouraged her to take a sabbatical to find out what she wants. She was only in her twenties but still at the crisis point. I challenged her to quit her job in three months. What she needs to do is give writing a shot. It may not pay well and may not work out, but she needs to know either way. She needs to live her best Childfree life, just like we all do.

While it is easy for me to spot when someone is at a crisis point, it is often harder to spot in yourself. Your partner, friends, or family may know when you are hitting the crisis point before you do (in fact, they usually do). Chances are that if you are hitting the Childfree Midlife Crisis, you have needed a change for a while. Ask your friends and family how long you have needed a change; you may be surprised by the answer. We all need to do a better job calling ourselves and others out when they need a change or are hitting a breaking point.

Not everyone can afford to take a sabbatical or to take a pay cut. If you are barely making ends meet or living paycheck to paycheck, it is not likely to be a choice. Yet for others, they may be able to make dramatic changes in spending in order to live the life they want to live. It may take downsizing your house or moving or doing something else, but it may be possible if you are creative and determined enough.

Working through a midlife crisis

Working through the Childfree Midlife Crisis will take personal, spiritual, and life/financial work. Get help. While some people can do this work alone, chances are you will make more progress with help. Depending on where you are in life and what you are struggling with, you will need one of three resources:

A therapist to help you look back

A spiritual person to help you look up and out

A coach or planner to help you look forward

Now I know these are generalizations, but the point is that you need to look back, up, and forward to work through the Childfree Midlife Crisis. Looking back can help you identify patterns, sources of your habits and anxieties, and more. When I say "looking up," I don't mean relying on religion specifically, but for some people, that fits. For others, looking up and out may be more about the bigger picture and the meaning of life or whatever spirituality means to them. Finally, a coach's or planner's job is to pat you on the back for what you have done and kick you in the butt to move forward.

You can either enlist professionals or use friends, books, or other options, but the bottom line is something needs to change. If you are working with a therapist and love it, you may need a coach (or vice versa). Whatever you like doing is probably not what you need to do.

Try to find professionals who understand what it means to be Childfree or Permanently Childless. Ask them how your plan changes because you are Childfree. If you are looking for a therapist or counselor, the *Tutum Journal* maintains a list of Childfree providers on their website. Finding spiritual support for being Childfree may be a bit more challenging, but that is where communities can help. If you need a coach or planner, contact us at Childfree Wealth®.

DIVING DEEPER: For more, visit https://childfreewealth.com/51.

FINANCIAL INDEPENDENCE, [YOU FILL IN THE BLANK]

Your approach to finances will change your life plan (and vice versa). At the core, you need to decide what role you want finances to play in your life. Do you want your finances to drive your life or your life to drive your finances? It may sound like semantics, but there is a vast difference. For example, I often work with people whose first question is "When can I retire?" My response is always the same: "Do you want to retire?" And their answer 95%+ of the time is some version of "Not really..." So, if retirement is not really their goal, why are they asking about it? Retirement is part of the Standard LifeScript and a way out of a job you don't love. Saving for retirement is one of those things you are "supposed" to do. After all, the goal of most financial plans is to retire. But what happens if you don't want to retire?

To be clear, there are two groups of people deciding not to retire. The first group includes people who enjoy what they do and want to do some version of it across their entire life. The second group includes people who will never be able to retire due to their financial situation and limitations in their environment. There is a big difference between choosing not to retire and being forced to work until you die. The challenge therefore is to figure out which you would prefer, and then plan for that.

What if instead of waiting until your elder years to do what you want, you did what brings you joy now? I'm not talking about going YOLO and ignoring everything. I'm talking about making purposeful decisions about what brings you joy and then making your finances fit them. If you have always wanted to open that cupcake shop, maybe you should. Or maybe work at the nonprofit that supports a cause you feel strongly about. You won't make as much money, but it is still possible. It may require making different life choices (maybe downsizing your expenditures and even your house), but would you be happier?

Financial Independence, Retire Early (FIRE)

The FIRE movement (Financial Independence, Retire Early) has taken off with younger generations, as the days of working twenty-five years to retire and get the watch are gone. Companies have little or no loyalty to their employees, and today employees are statistically best off if they move to a new job every three years or so (which tends to result in higher pay over time). Pensions are unheard of outside of academia and government work. U.S. Social Security is at risk. The bottom line is our retirement plans are up to each of us and the choices we make.

The concept of FIRE is simple: scrimp and save now so you can retire early. Some people take FIRE to extremes by living on ramen noodles and making their own soap now to retire ASAP. The challenge is that many people know what they want to retire *from* but don't have as clear a picture of what they want to retire *to*. What you do in retirement can impact your social, mental, and physical health. It is okay to do whatever you want in retirement, but you need *something* to do.

There are many levels of FIRE to consider, and new ones seem to be coming out daily:

Lean FIRE: Retiring on expenses that are as low as possible (as if you are living on ramen noodles for your entire life).

Chubby FIRE: Retiring to a nice lifestyle. Not rich, not poor (as if you can afford to go out to eat when you want to).

Fat FIRE: Living it up in retirement (as if you have a private chef).

Coast or Slow FIRE: Trying to find a balance between saving now and retiring in the future. Not overexerting yourself now to retire as early as possible, but just putting your time in.

Barista FIRE: Retiring and then working a job for benefits or social interaction.

Determining a rough FIRE number for you can be easy. FIRE proponents often follow the research on a safe withdrawal rate (SWR) in retirement of 4% (more on this later in the retirement chapter). The SWR says you can take out 4% of your net worth each year over a thirty-year retirement period and be okay most of the time. So, if you have a $1 million net worth, you can take out $40K each year in retirement. The inverse says that you can find your FIRE number if you take your annual expenses now and multiply them by twenty-five (i.e., if you have $40K in expenses, your FIRE number is $1 million).

FIRE numbers are rough math and don't consider taxes, inflation, and many other factors, but they give you an idea of when you can retire if retirement is your goal.

DIVING DEEPER: For more, visit https://childfreewealth.com/54.

Financial Independence, Live Early (FILE)

For Childfree people who want an alternative to FIRE, I encourage them to consider living a Financial Independence, Live Early (FILE) lifestyle. If FIRE is an on/off switch for work, FILE is more of a dimmer switch reflecting doing the right work, at the right time, and in the right amounts across your life. FILE focuses on maximizing joy in your life across your lifespan rather than just in retirement. Here's an example.

I interviewed my client Ryan for my book *Portraits of Childfree Wealth*. Ryan and his wife are Childfree and had retired early. When he retired, he found that he was bored and unfulfilled. He came out of retirement and opened his own marketing company. Ryan set hard-and-fast rules that he never works before 10:00 a.m., does not work more than twenty-five hours a week, and never works on Fridays. He also works remotely, and you will find him working from across the world. That is living the FILE lifestyle.

I have found that most Childfree people would work for as long as they can, as long as they were doing something they enjoy. It is common to see Childfree people open their own businesses to have that flexibility. They may make less in their business, but they are happier. Others will arrange for flexible work schedules or part-time work, so they can do what they enjoy. Many travel regularly, and some do not even have a regular home.

I'll call out the editor of this book here as a great example. She works in publishing, but she is somewhere different every time I see her via Zoom. For two years, Erin and her dog, Cheddar, stayed in Airbnb rentals across the United States, enjoying a work-life balance many can only hope to attain. Since she is in publishing, she needs to have storage for all her books, but that is no big deal. She enjoys what she does and lives her best Childfree life by her own rules.

FIRE fans have said that FILE is just Barista FIRE or Coast FIRE. The similarities are there, but the difference is that retirement is never truly a goal with FILE. I could argue, and have, that if you are working in retirement, you aren't retired (i.e., Barista FIRE isn't really retirement).

One of my colleagues, Cody Garrett, CFP®, founder of Measure Twice Planning, calls FIRE *Financial Independence, Recreational Employment,* which is closer to FILE.

The terms matter less than the general concepts. The question to ask yourself is whether you want to retire and not work ever again or whether you would rather do something you enjoy, maybe as an encore career. There is a massive difference between *having* to work in retirement and *choosing* to work in retirement. I once worked at a florist doing deliveries. It was a great job, as people are always happy when they get flowers. I would consider doing that in retirement just to get out of the house, but not because I had to pay the bills with it.

Living a FILE lifestyle will shift your priorities and your investments. Rather than investing for retirement, you can invest in yourself and what brings you joy. You could decide to take a six-month sabbatical and invest in finding yourself. You could invest in starting a new business or going back to school. You could move to an area you enjoy. The options are endless.

DIVING DEEPER: For more, visit https://childfreewealth.com/53.

Financial Independence (FI)

The core of FIRE and FILE is the same: FI, which stands for financial independence. You may have heard of FI as getting to the point of having "F-You money." When you have F-You money, you can tell your boss what to do with their job and not worry about the repercussions. You can move 1,200 miles away (as my wife and I did) for a new career. You can take chances, fail, and still be okay. You can do what you want and enjoy it.

Achieving financial independence may seem like a pipe dream to many, but it is possible. The key to FI is to keep a focus on the basics: getting on a budget, paying down debt, and saving and investing. Just because they are basics does not mean they are easy. However, you can get to FI by diligently honoring the basics year after year—after that, financial independence is just a matter of time. Don't let your current financial situation cloud your vision for the future.

The bonus is that once you achieve financial independence, you can choose to live early, retire early, or combine both. With FI, you get to use the time and freedom that come with being Childfree to do whatever you want. It goes back to that first Kinder question on page 19 that you journaled about: What would you do if you were financially independent?

Rent and ramen

When it comes to jobs, there are two phases: the rent-and-ramen phase and the rest of your life. When you are in the rent-and-ramen phase, you are living paycheck to paycheck, barely making enough money to cover the basics. The struggle is real, and you will likely have to take any job you can get. The challenge is that many live their entire lives as if stuck in the rent-and-ramen phase. Something needs to change.

Housing in the United States is prohibitively expensive, especially if you are single. Inflation and lifestyle creep can eat whatever is left over in your paycheck, and you can feel like you have no options. You may get stuck on the hedonic treadmill, or as I call it, "the gerbil wheel." As your expenses increase, you need to work more or do work you don't want to do just to make ends meet. Eventually, you get decades into your career, look back, and ask yourself, *How did I get here?* Or, more critically, *How do I get out?*

The key to financial happiness is to either want less stuff or to make more money. The problem is that our society, and social media in particular, pushes us to compare ourselves against others, leaving us to feel like we are lacking if we don't have that big house, nice car, or whatever. The thing about social media is that you may see the nice car they just got, but no one shows the $700-per-month car payment that goes with it. Many (or most) of us suffer from comparing ourselves with others, even though we live a completely different life plan. As the old proverb goes, "Comparison is the thief of joy."

DIVING DEEPER: For more, visit https://childfreewealth.com/63.

PICKING THE "RIGHT" CAREER

If you can step off the gerbil wheel and stop comparing yourself to others, you can choose a different path for your life. It may go against everything you have been taught, but taking a cut in pay is okay in order to be happier doing something else. It is also okay to do something completely different from what you went to school for. It is okay to choose to be happy at work rather than taking a big enough paycheck to be miserable at work. When you are struggling to make ends meet, this may sound crazy, and it is. The key is to create a plan to solidify your finances so that you can follow joy, not just the mighty dollar.

We all have limited time on this earth, and most people spend a third of their time at work. If you spend a third of your life doing something, it should bring you joy. For many people, that is a foreign concept, but it is possible to get fulfillment and joy from what you do. It may not be possible on the path you are on now, but it is possible. Every day, I get to help people achieve their dreams and goals. It is like I'm being paid to play baseball. I even do it for free when people need help and I have the time. What would you be willing to do for free that you can still get paid for?

Taking a sabbatical

Figuring out what you want to be when you grow up or finding something you would do for free can be challenging if you are stuck on the gerbil wheel. We get so stuck on our career path that we often can't even stop and think about anything else. Many people just keep doing what they are "supposed to do" until they have a significant life event, like a heart attack, that shocks them into thinking differently. Rather than waiting for that life event, maybe you should consider taking a sabbatical.

Sabbaticals are popular in academia, and some businesses have embraced the concept. At its core, a sabbatical is time off work to recenter and refresh yourself. Most of us are not lucky enough to take a paid sabbatical from work, but we can still choose to take one on our own dime. I recommend a six-month sabbatical (or similar) if you can afford it. Here's a plan for structuring your sabbatical for maximum impact:

First two months: Watch Netflix, Hulu, or whatever mindless activity you like. The intent of the first two months is to allow you to decompress from years on the gerbil wheel.

Second two months: Figure out what you want to do when you grow up. The intent is to take two months to envision a different life. What have you always wanted to do but were too afraid to try?

Last two months: Try it out. With an idea in place, here is your opportunity to try it out. Maybe take an internship or a class or just talk to people in that field. The point is to try it before you dive in completely.

I'm willing to bet that if you take six months off to figure out what you want to do, the answer will not be to go back to what you were doing. It may be, but I have yet to see that in practice. I've worked with many people who took a sabbatical, and the result is often completely different from where they were. I've had people write that novel they always wanted to write, hike the Appalachian Trail, go back to school, form a nonprofit, and do a wide variety of other activities. The thing they all say is that it was a life-changing experience and well worth the cost.

Think of the cost of a sabbatical as an investment in you. There is the direct cost of not having a paycheck for six months and the indirect cost of starting something new. If you have a partner, you may be able to swing the costs of living on one salary. If you are single, you need to plan a bit more. You are financially ready to take a sabbatical when you have no debts and six to twelve months of normal expenses in addition to your emergency fund.

Keep your eyes open for risk-free opportunities to take a sabbatical. You may be able to volunteer for a layoff or a "phased retirement" at work to get what is effectively a paid-for sabbatical. Some companies will even offer for you to take six months of unpaid leave, with a job waiting for you when you're done. But be careful with that, as the temptation of a job waiting for you may distract you from being creative about what you want.

DIVING DEEPER: For more, visit https://childfreewealth.com/64.

Choosing a career

I always loved those career aptitude tests in high school because you could game them to make sure they say you should be an astronaut. Even though I got the test to say I should be an astronaut, NASA never called me (and I never made it to space camp). The thought that we might know what we want to do for fifty-plus years at eighteen years old is laughable at best. My sister and I were the first in our family to go to college, and if you told eighteen-year-old me that I'd have a PhD and an MBA, I would have never believed you. So why do many of us allow our choices from decades ago to drive our career choices now?

The reality is that many adults never really picked their career path. Instead, they were told they would be good at X, or should go to school for Y, or should do as their family member did and become Z. Then they head off to college, change majors a few times, and end up on a "career path." Once you are on a path, opportunities come, and you end up stuck moving up the ladder (or to other jobs in the same career path). After a decade or so on that path, it becomes almost unthinkable to start over. The only responsible answer is to keep working hard until you retire.

We need to throw out all that head trash—the decisions made for us by our family and made by our younger, dumber selves. Depending on whose statistics you follow, we will each have three to seven significant career changes in our life. Note that it is *career* changes, not job changes. If you haven't tried a new career, you are obviously holding back the average for the rest of us (just joking, kinda). The key is to understand why people make career changes. All too often, it is for more money. My challenge to you is to make a career change for more joy, and if it pays you well, all the better!

I made my first million before I was twenty-one and spent it by the age of twenty-five (what else would you expect a twenty-one-year-old to do with a million dollars?). I did some good things with the money to help my family. I also spent a bunch of it on stuff I didn't need, like an old-school, original Hummer. Lots of fun. What I can tell you is that it is true that money does not buy happiness, but it does make it feel like the work is worth it.

The trap to watch out for is when you are working just to make money to get away from your job. I always hear from people who say they have to make more money to support their lifestyle. I will pull apart their lifestyle and find that they're undertaking a considerable amount of retail therapy to deal with the stress of their job. Or they are truly working and living just for their time off. Sound familiar?

Something needs to change, or you will find yourself a decade older and deeper in a career you don't want to be in. And watch out for magic numbers. I regularly have people tell me that if they could just make $100K a year (or some other number), their life and financial problems would fix themselves. Spoiler alert: they won't. Your personal money behaviors and relationship with your job need to change—not the dollar signs—for you to be happy.

Owning a small business

What happens if, after your soul searching, you decide you want to start a small business (or even a medium-large business) or a nonprofit? Or maybe you want to monetize your side hustle? You are in for a rough awakening, but it is okay because many of us are doing the same thing. Running a small business can be both immensely rewarding and unbelievably frustrating.

As I tell my wife, I work for a crazy person (me) who never stops thinking about his business and won't settle for anything less than perfection. My current boss sets obnoxious goals (like writing this book) and then beats me up if anything goes wrong. It would be so much easier to work for someone else, but then I wouldn't be able to choose my own adventure, and the likelihood of a big company allowing me to serve Childfree and Permanently Childless people is near zero.

I wish I had Ryan's ability to set hard-and-fast boundaries for my own business. I asked him what happens if a client wants to meet on Friday, his promised day off, or before 10:00 a.m. He explained he had one customer who pushed that boundary, and he fired the customer. I'm getting better at keeping the weekends to myself, but when a customer genuinely needs me, I still have trouble saying no. Finding a balance and living a FILE lifestyle is challenging but rewarding.

Starting a business is easier than ever, but is it worth it? The challenge is that worth depends on what measure you use. I often use the McDonald's test when it comes to actual dollars. With the McDonald's test, you figure out how much you are making per hour from the business, and if you are making less than your local McDonald's is paying, you are better off working there. The problem with the McDonald's test is that it does not measure joy. It also does not set an appropriate value on your time, business, and what you give to the world.

I did a series of financial planning sessions with Anna from the *We're Not Kidding* podcast that I shared on our *Childfree Wealth*® podcast. Anna's focus is to help people through the choice to be Childfree and to live their best life. In our first sessions, she admitted that she struggles, as her business does not make as much money as she wants. When we dove deeper, we found that Anna, like many others, valued herself by how much she made. By the measure of the McDonald's test, she was not doing well. Instead of focusing on the revenue or dollars, we shifted to setting goals on the number of lives impacted as her true north. As a couple, Anna and her husband, Grant, could afford for Anna to focus on impact rather than adding for Anna to focus on making an impact rather than having more money to the bank.

BUSINESS BASICS

If you start your own business, you have two tasks: providing the service or goods you want to sell and running the company. It is common for people to want to start a business, such as making decorated flowerpots, without knowing how to run the company. Effectively, you will need to set two goals: one monetary and the other based upon your joy or impact (whatever matters most to you). Chances are the joy or impact measure will come from what you do, while the monetary goal reflects running the business itself.

It does not matter if you are starting a nonprofit or a for-profit company; you still need to watch the financial bottom line. As was drilled into my head in nonprofit healthcare, no margin equals no mission. That's a nice way of saying that if you don't have a profit, you won't be able to keep running the business (even if it is a nonprofit). For a basic primer on profit and accounting, pick up the book *Profit First* by Mike Michalowicz. You don't need a wacky accounting system. You just need to make sure you are at least breaking even.

STARTING OFF SMALL

The best thing to do when starting a business is to start off small, with a minimum viable product (MVP). The key is to get your product or service out there and see how it goes. If you are starting a flowerpot business, you might start by doing small batches and selling them locally on Facebook. You don't even need a website at this point. You just need to get started. You also don't have to worry too much about making a profit (yet); just set a maximum budget you can afford to spend on the attempt.

If you are still working a job at this stage, keep it. Build up the business to a point where it is stable enough that you can drop your job and make a slide over. This may mean working two full-time jobs for a while, but with the number of businesses that fail, it is worth giving it a trial run first.

Grow your business at the speed of cash. Do not borrow money to start a business. When you borrow money for your business, you will most likely have to guarantee it personally. In plain language, that means that if your business does not work out, you will still be stuck with the debt. Start small and reinvest your profits back into the business.

SO, DO YOU STILL WANT TO START A BUSINESS?

I just outlined the basics of starting and running a business to give you a flavor of what it is like. If you still have the passion for starting a business or monetizing a side hustle, set a goal to start it within thirty days. Don't worry about getting it "right." Set a budget for how much money you can spend on it, and consider it no differently than any other discretionary spending.

The key with a business is to try things. You will fail and make mistakes, but the difference between success and failure is how quickly you pick yourself up and try something else. That does not mean trying a whole new business when you hit a speed bump but trying a different path, product, or service toward the same end.

DIVING DEEPER: For more, visit https://childfreewealth.com/57.

SETTING BOUNDARIES IN CARING FOR ELDERLY FAMILY MEMBERS

When I was sixteen years old, my mother had her first heart attack. I vividly remember having to call 911, and the night it happened is burned into my brain. That night is important, because it was the turning point for my mother's health, and not for the better. Since then, she has been disabled, and caring for her in one way or another has been part of my life for decades. While my sister and I take turns by splitting responsibilities and more, it is still a challenge at times.

I know I'm not alone. The sandwich generation—people taking care of their parents and kids at the same time—is growing, and as

Childfree people, we are the open-faced sandwich (taking care of our parents, without kids). It goes this way: "You don't have kids so you can take care of <fill in the blank>." We are often expected to take care of our elderly family members, which is probably not fair. But fair or not, we still need a plan.

You will find caring for elderly family members in both the life planning section of this book and financial planning, and that is intentional. Before you create a plan, you need good, hard boundaries for what you will and won't do for your family members. For example, my wife and I have a hard boundary that no one lives with us. I also won't give money to family members. These boundaries may seem harsh, but they are there to protect us and our life.

The challenge with setting any boundaries is that while you get to pick your boundaries, you have no control over others' reactions to those boundaries. It is easier to set a boundary well in advance of an emergency than to try to set up a structure when your loved one is hurt or in crisis. While I won't give money to family members directly, I will pay for an Instacart delivery of groceries, or pay a medical bill for them. I don't give money because it will drive me crazy if they spend it frivolously, but I do want to help. I have figured out ways to respect my own boundaries while helping them.

Take a moment and ask yourself these questions:

Who is going to expect me to care for them?

What am I willing to do (or not do) for them?

Am I willing to have them move in with me or me to move in with them?

How much of my own personal finances am I willing to spend on them?

How can I support them indirectly, and is that better for me?

Caregiving is hard and can be expensive. Not everyone is cut out to handle it. Even if you work in a caring profession (e.g., a nurse or other caregiver), that does not mean you can handle your own family member being sick. I had to call 911 when my mother had her heart attack because my father was a wreck. Mind you, my father served for decades in the local volunteer fire department helping others and was even fire chief for a while. He just couldn't handle his wife being sick.

Caregiving costs both time and money. If you have more money than time, you may want to look at enlisting a team of caregivers to help both you and your loved one. We will dive further into this in the finances section, but you should know there are options to provide care without doing it directly.

The bottom line is that caring for family members could have more of an impact on your life and finances than many other choices you make. If you have a partner, or have parents who are divorced, you may have a wide range of people to take care of. You may have to make some hard choices in your career and housing to live near them. You may have to take a leave from work to care for them. You may have to spend a large amount of your money on their care. If you don't set boundaries upfront, you may lose yourself, and that is the opposite of living your best life.

DIVING DEEPER: For more, visit https://childfreewealth.com/23.

3

IF YOU'RE A SOLOIST (AKA SOLO-AGING)

Why did you decide to be Childfree?

"I am kind of an extreme introvert and I really need my alone time to feel relaxed and at peace. (I am also happily single.) Kids are very demanding, and I am sure I would turn into a mental health wreck if I had to deal with kids all the time, even if they were also introverts. And, of course, there's no guarantee about personality if I were to have kids. I don't even have pets because I just don't want to be responsible for the care and well-being of another creature in my house."

—KAYLA, THIRTY-EIGHT, SINGLE

While I'm not sure I 100% love the term, technically if you are single and don't have kids, you are a "solo-ager" or are "solo-aging," or my favorite term—a "soloist." I will use the terms *solo-aging* and *soloist* here, as they reflect terms that may be helpful if you go down the google rabbit hole and want more support. Note that you can be in your twenties and still be considered to be solo-aging, as you are still getting older. Some may look at the term and assume an older age (and it is sometimes used that way), but it reflects the life cycle of being single and Childfree or Childless.

Solo-aging is much like being Childfree, in that some people choose to be single, and for others it is not by choice. Dating while being Childfree brings its own challenges, which are a topic for another book and another author. The one thing to keep in mind is that if you want to find a partner or group to be with, that should be part of your life plan. If you have been telling yourself that you are too busy to date or find a friend group, that may need to change. If you are happy living the single life, all the more power to you!

The bonus of a solo-ager is that you get to do whatever you want without someone else weighing in. The downside is that you don't have someone else to weigh in or to share costs with. There are times when having an accountability partner will be important, so you may need to find a friend or professional to be that sounding board for you. For example, when you are budgeting, it is very easy to justify your mindless spending without someone to provide accountability. One of my first clients had a problem with ordering DoorDash too frequently. It wasn't until I helped her look at the total amount she was spending per year that she realized that it was holding her back from her goals, like travel. I was very proud of her when she canceled her DashPass membership and focused on her fun travel plans! You can choose to spend your money however you want, but if it is holding you back from doing what brings you joy, it may need to shift, and you might not be able to do that alone.

THE SOLO TAX

The single tax may be proverbial and not levied by the IRS, but it is a real thing. A study by Fidelity estimates that it costs between $480,000 and $1 million in additional costs across a soloist's life.[5] Housing in the United States is expensive, and it is a lot cheaper if you can split it. Same goes for cars. And groceries. And utilities. And travel. Even streaming

5 Deanna Lauder, "A Family of One: The Ascendance of Solo Households," Fidelity Center for Applied Technology, March 27, 2023, https://fcatalyst.com/blog/march2023/a-family-of-one-the-ascendence-of-solo-households.

services are cheaper if you can split them. I know Netflix now forbids it, but they used to say that love is sharing a password. The bottom line is that it can be expensive to be single, so you need to keep an eye on your budget.

Housing deserves a special callout here. There is an entire chapter about the decision to buy a house or not later in the book, but solo-agers need to think a bit differently. With rising housing costs, I've seen quite a few people consider co-housing in some form or another. It might look like having a roommate or having the classic *Golden Girls* setup. The best I ever heard was from a widow who wanted to buy a castle for her and all her friends to live out their later years. It sounds a bit drafty to me, but I do love castles! In addition to splitting costs, sharing space can provide help for household chores, maintenance, and more.

If you are going to share housing costs (and space), look at the chapters on planning as a couple or group. It does not matter if you are sharing with a spouse or a platonic friend; you need to have appropriate paperwork to protect everyone involved.

Sharing space is not for everyone, and if you want to live alone, you will just have to plan for that cost. Finding reasonable housing that you can afford as a soloist can be a challenge. You may have to live farther away from the city center, or in an area with fewer amenities in order to find lower cost housing. Of course, this comes with a trade-off. If you work from home, and plan to forever, you can always look at sites like MakeMyMove for areas willing to pay you to move there. Yes, they exist, but they may not be in places you want to move to.

As a soloist, you may also want to take a good look at fifty-five-and-older communities, once you've hit that threshold. These communities often offer townhouse or condo-like living, with additional communal services, including recreation, food services, and more. Depending on the area, they may be a reasonably priced option. If you are not fifty-five yet, they may still be an option, as many communities can allow up to 20% of residents to be younger than fifty-five years old. I always thought these communities would be great for Childfree people, and my wife and I would love to live in one.

WHAT HAPPENS TO YOUR STUFF WHEN YOU'RE GONE

Solo-aging provides some unique planning opportunities when it comes to estate planning. Estate planning includes what happens to your stuff after you pass but also who is going to make decisions for you (wills, living wills, power of attorney, etc.). Couples often have a built-in person who can make decisions for them that solo-agers do not. If you are not close to your family or if you don't have a friend you would trust, take a special look at page 175 where I explain establishing a Childfree Trust. You can pay someone to be your executor or have power of attorney, which might be a great option for you.

Take special care to make sure your healthcare directives (living will) and power of attorney documents are very detailed about your wishes. If you do not have an advocate at your bedside when you need one, these documents may help. Make sure your healthcare directives are on file with your primary care physician and put into your electronic medical record. If you are reading this, you need to stop and get that paperwork done and filed, no matter what age you are.

Solo-agers often worry about who to give their money to. First, I want you to consider the *Die With Zero* approach. If your plan has you dying with a bunch of money, it may need some adjustments now. You might be able to shift how much you work, or how you spend your money to get more joy out of your life rather than just building a big bank account. Don't worry—we are still going to make sure you don't run out of money, but at the same time you don't want to die with millions in the bank.

If you are going to have a lot to give at the end of your life, you might want to consider whose life you could improve now. Giving while you are alive is a great way to handle your estate. You can do whatever you want with your money. If you want to leave it all to your pets (and whoever cares for them), that is fine. If you want to give it to family, friends, or anyone else, that is your choice. Just be careful not to let people have a vote on what you do with your money when they might be the recipients (i.e., if you ask your nephew what to do with your money, he might tell you to give it all to him).

"BUT WHO IS GOING TO TAKE CARE OF YOU WHEN YOU'RE OLD?"

While most Childfree and Childless people have heard the question, "Who is going to take care of you when you are old?" solo-agers tend to feel this question a bit more acutely. If you are worried about who is going to take care of you in your elder years, it is a valid question that you need to answer. Be sure to check page 159, which explains long-term care options, but keep in mind that long-term care insurance is most expensive for single women. Part of this is because women use 3.7 years of care, while men use 2.2 years on average. Couples get a break on long-term care insurance, because there is an assumption that their partner will care for them for a while. Solo-agers need to both have a financial solution for long-term care and appropriate paperwork in place.

Your aim should be to have a plan in place for long-term care by your midforties. If you are past that, it is okay; start now. If you are still in your thirties, it depends on how much you worry about the long-term care question. I've had people who just turned thirty get quotes on long-term care insurance, but few take it up. If it is bothering you, paying for long-term care insurance might be a great way to get rid of the fear by paying someone else—your insurance provider—to worry about it for you.

One of the bonuses of considering a fifty-five-and-older community is that many of them are part of a network of aging care facilities that include in-home, assisted living, and long-term care options, possibly on the same campus. There is even a trend of turning old malls into these communities, which sounds like a novel solution. The bonus to you is that as you age you can get just the help you need, no more and no less. You may have to do a bit of searching, but you will find these communities—often called "villages"—and you may be surprised to find how nice some are (even if they aren't cheap).

YOU CAN'T DO IT ALL ALONE

As a soloist, you need to know when to ask for help. This could be everything from household help (cleaning, landscaping, maintenance, etc.) to financial, legal, and medical help, and more. For example, you will need to enlist either a family member or a professional to serve as your medical and financial power of attorney. You need someone who can make decisions for you when you can't. Don't be shy about asking for (and paying for) help. It is yet another single tax, but you only have so many hours in the day and will need to pay for help just to make it through. Budget appropriately, and sometimes it can even be more economical to pay for help than to do it yourself. I don't enjoy mowing the lawn, so I pay someone to do it for me. The reality is that I can pick up an extra hour or two of work and pay for Joey to do my landscaping, and he does a better job than I do (and I don't have to fight with my allergies).

DIVING DEEPER: For more, visit https://childfreewealth.com/20.

4
FINANCIAL PLANNING AS A COUPLE

What are your goals?

"Start my own business, but not sure how to do it. My husband wants to work until sixty-five and I want to be a stay-at-home wife with my own business."

—BLOSSOM, FORTY-NINE, MARRIED

There are two questions I regularly get from couples: Should we combine finances? and Should we get married? My answer to both of these questions is annoying: "It depends..." I will address the marriage question a bit later, but let's dig into combining finances. The key to this question is not about if you are combining accounts but if you are doing financial planning together.

How many financial plans are you working on as a couple? While you each may have your own life plan (which may differ at points), a couple can have one, two, or three financial plans going at any time:

Everything combined (one plan): The bonus of combining everything is that you both work on the same financial goals. The downside is that some people feel a loss of identity or the ability to do things on their own (but this can be addressed).

Everything separate (two plans): If you are each creating your own plan, it is like you are roommates. The benefit is that you each get to control your own future. The downside is that you are not truly working together on your goals, and conflicting goals may actually negatively affect of you.

Yours, mine, and ours (three plans): I call this "hybrid financial planning." As a couple you might have a shared financial plan and finances around the house (or other goals), yet you keep your own finances and goals for everything else. The benefit is that you are working together on some goals. The downside is that inequalities in income and spending can become an issue.

I'm intentionally talking about combining finances before the debate on getting married, as this should be a discussion well before you get married. We each bring with us different values, experiences, and knowledge in regards to money. Money is the second most common cause of divorce in the United States (just behind infidelity—and financial infidelity also exists). You want to have the money discussions early and often as a couple. You not only want to talk about whether you want to combine finances and how, but you also want to share your credit reports early on (you show me yours, I'll show you mine).

The actual numbers around finances tend to have less of an impact than a mismatch of values. Widely varying net worth, income, or credit scores may not be an issue if you are on the same page after you discuss and disclose everything. The issue comes when you have differing money values. For example, I worked with a couple who was just engaged. They wanted to combine finances and buy a house. As we worked together, it quickly became evident that one person lived a debt-free life, and the other loved debt, credit cards, and loans. If they combined finances, it would be a long time before the debt was paid off and they would be able to buy a house. It also demonstrated that they have completely different spending and saving habits. In the end, the couple was not able to reconcile the money differences and called off the marriage. While I consider myself pretty good at helping to facilitate healthy money discussions in a couple, they were just too far apart and unwilling to budge in their own stances.

TALK IT OUT

It is no surprise that communication is at the core of a healthy relationship, and that goes double for finances. In coaching, they say you can't coach someone who has seen you naked or whom you have seen naked. That means it is going to be tough to teach your spouse or family members about finance. I help people with their finances for a living and still can't teach my wife or mother anything. With that in mind, I want you each to blame me, not each other, for any money discussions (or fights). Feel free to say, "Dr. Jay says we need to talk about these questions" and then dig in. You can either journal your answers to these questions, or take turns with who answers each question first (i.e., your spouse gives their answer first, then you give your opinion, then you switch):

What does your life plan look like? Go into as much detail as possible. Use the Kinder questions on page 19 as a place to start.

What are your goals and dreams in life? Pay attention to goals and dreams that were not part of the life plan.

What are your boundaries with money and life? A great example is the boundary that my mom isn't moving in with us during her elder years.

What was money like for you growing up? Our experiences with money in the past often color our future with money.

What does your credit report look like, and how do you feel about debt? The score itself (or total dollar amount of debt) doesn't matter as much as a comparison of values around money.

What do you like to spend money on? It is common for people to spend money differently, and someone in the couple may focus on quantity (lots of small things) while the other person focuses on quality (one big thing).

What impact is your family going to have on our money? Will one person need to support their family financially, and/or is there an inheritance coming?

How much money do you have, and how much do you make? At some point, you should both know the numbers, including net worth and income.

Do you think you should combine finances? If so, are you combining completely or doing a hybrid approach?

If those questions seem daunting, or you have been a couple for years and never discussed any of it, it is time to have a real conversation. You may want to (or need to) enlist professional help to facilitate the discussion. Depending on how far apart you are and how deep you want to go, you might want to talk to a financial therapist or a CERTIFIED FINANCIAL PLANNER™. Grab a couple of hours (or more) with either and work through the debate about combining finances. It may not be pleasant upfront, but it is critical when it comes to life and financial planning.

I worked with a couple who had gotten into their sixties before they ever talked about finances. They had done fine planning individually up until the point of retirement. Moving to a fixed income challenged everything. We were able to work through it and they did well, but I can't count how many times they said they wished they had talked about finances earlier.

Now, I know at this point you want a definitive answer to the question of whether to combine finances, and I'm not going to give you one—sorry! There are way too many factors that go into the decision. If you are on the same page financially, with the same goals and good communication, you are probably better off combining finances. You can combine your checking and savings accounts, but keep in mind that your retirement accounts will still be individual. Just be sure the beneficiaries on each of your retirement accounts are set appropriately.

One relationship saver if you combine finances is pocket money. In your budget, be sure to plan for each person to have their own pocket money. This money can be spent however they want, and the other person has no say. If one person wants to spend it all on small items, and the other person wants to save their pocket money for a big purchase, that is fine. Having pocket money is a relationship saver—and it allows you to buy gifts for each other.

MARRIED (OR NOT) WITHOUT CHILDREN

The second question I'm going to dodge a bit is: Should we get married? The answer is less about finances and much more about life, romance, religion, culture, and other issues that I am not going to try to tackle. Marriage is a choice, not a requirement, for Childfree and Childless people. I am going to try to give you some things to think about in regards to marriage. Just keep in mind that I'm coming at it completely from a financial standpoint, not an emotional one.

Healthcare benefits

Qualifying for healthcare benefits is probably the most common reason I hear for why Childfree people are getting married. It is a good reason, generally, because most employers do not offer benefits to long-term partners who are not married. I hope this changes in the future, but as of right now, you need to be married to benefit from your partner's benefits. Watch out, as some employers charge more for spousal insurance than it would cost you to get a plan on the healthcare marketplace.

Citizenship

Some couples get married for citizenship purposes. In many cases, citizenship by marriage is the easiest way to address visa issues or other complex immigration questions. Just remember that this comes with scrutiny from the government, and they are likely to want to see that you combine finances (among other things) to prove it was not just a "paper marriage." If you are working on citizenship issues, you need to contact an immigration attorney for guidance.

Wills, powers of attorney (POAs), and other paperwork

Getting married provides you some automatic protections when it comes to wills, estates, medical decision-making, and more. Each state has its own guidelines. If you are not going to get married, you need to make sure you have appropriate paperwork, including a will, power of attorney (POA), partnership agreement (for buying a house or similar), and other pertinent documents. You should also have a will and POA if you are married, but at least you have some governmental protection already built in by the very fact that you are married.

Taxes

Keep in mind that once you get married, you *must* file your taxes together. You can either file Married or Married Filing Separate, but you can no longer file as Single. In some cases, you will pay more as a married couple, and other times you will not. (It is confusing, I know.) Your tax filing may also impact your student loans if you are on an income-based repayment plan, and you may need to file Married Filing Separate to keep your payments lower, even if it raises your taxes slightly.

Debt

It is possible to get a mortgage as an unmarried couple, but being married tends to make it easier. When you apply for debt as a married couple, the lower credit score of the two of you will be the one they use, but they will use your combined income, which may help you qualify. Any debt you sign for together will be the responsibility of both you and your spouse, so be aware.

Social Security

If you are married, you may be able to claim a spousal benefit for Social Security. Where this tends to help is if one person made significantly more money than the other. The spouse who made less may be able to claim off their spouse's higher Social Security calculation, and it does not impact the higher earning spouse at all.

Gifting

I don't want to get too far into this, but married spouses are allowed to gift each other an unlimited amount, while there is a gift limit each year ($18,000 in 2024) for non-married couples before the gift is taxed by the IRS. Talk to your CPA for more information, especially if either of you has a considerable net worth or is expecting a large inheritance.

Community property states

Another quirk to keep in mind is that nine states are community property states: Arizona, California, Idaho, Louisiana, Nevada, New Mexico, Texas, Washington, and Wisconsin. In community property states, all property, income, and debt are treated as if it is owned 50/50. Most commonly, being in a community property state impacts estate planning and divorce. If you are in one of these states, you will probably want to read up a bit more about how it works.

DIVING DEEPER: For more, visit https://childfreewealth.com/22.

IF YOU ARE NOT GOING TO GET MARRIED

If you are in a long-term relationship but not getting married, you need to meet with an attorney and a CERTIFIED FINANCIAL PLANNER™ to make sure you have the right paperwork in place. Before you buy a property together, or do finances together, you need a partnership agreement or something similar in place to make sure you are protected. If you own a home and don't have a partnership agreement or will, you may be homeless if your partner passes. Your agreement should discuss how to dissolve the partnership, just as if it were a business. Each state has its own quirks, so make sure to meet with a local attorney to determine what you need to get done.

DIVING DEEPER: For more, visit https://childfreewealth.com/21.

THE GARDENER AND THE ROSE

One of the benefits that come from being a DINK couple is that you may be able to embrace the Gardener and the Rose concept. I've seen many couples successfully embrace this approach, including my wife and me. Here are the basics:

The Gardener: Provides support so that the Rose can grow. Support can come in many forms, ranging from literal gardening to housekeeping, emotional support, financial support, and more.

The Rose: Has an opportunity to grow with the support of the Gardener. Growth may include taking a sabbatical, going back to school, changing careers, starting a business, finding themselves, or any other growth opportunity.

You may have heard of this approach before as the Gardener and the Flower. When my wife and I decided to embrace this approach,

I decided she wasn't just any flower, she is a rose, hence why I have renamed the entire process.

The bonus of this approach is that there are defined roles, and both people are working on the same set of goals, even if it is in a different way. One rule I try to set is that there must be a time limit to the arrangement, and then roles reverse. Having a time limit allows both people to focus on their roles and on themselves. It is easier in many cases to be the Gardener than the Rose. The Rose often feels selfish, but that is okay, because that is intentional, as it is time limited.

My story

My wife and I are both PhDs. The challenge with having two PhDs in a couple is that it is nearly impossible to find two equal careers, in specialized fields, at the same time, and in the same location. In academia, they even have human resources policies to handle the "trailing spouse" and "spousal hires" to address this issue. The trailing spouse may be offered what seems like a consolation job to recruit the person they really want. (I really don't like the concept and implications of the trailing spouse, and the connotation that they are less than, but here we are.)

To get around these issues, my wife and I embraced the Gardener and the Rose. I was on a path to be a healthcare executive for life before I hit my Childfree Midlife Crisis point. By pure luck, my wife had finished her PhD around that time, so it became a great time to make her the Rose. We talked about it, and she went on the job market and found a tenure-track faculty job. (For those outside of academia, getting a tenure-track faculty job is a great, and rare, accomplishment.)

To fast-forward a bit, we ended up having to move twice, with the last move being a 1,200-mile move to Mississippi. I freely admit that Mississippi was never even on my list of potential states to move to, but she got a great job here. (In hindsight, running a financial planning firm focused on helping Childfree and Childless people in a post–*Roe v. Wade* world, in Mississippi, was not ideal, to say the least.) My wife is doing great, and I work hard to support her. I make sure the house is taken care of, cook, pay the bills, and help her in any way I can with her job. The focus is all on her succeeding, so if that means she needs help with a research project or a grant or just moving books, I'm there. I intentionally opened my own company so that I have the flexibility to support her.

We have agreed that in ten to fifteen years, I will get to be the Rose. When I'm the Rose, we are getting in a boat (my goal is a Nordhavn 51, a *very* nice boat) and traveling the world. She can choose if she continues to work remotely or not but it will be my turn to grow. (Note: My turn is not about growing financially, but about growing rich in experiences. If I had my choice, I'd be a boat captain for a living—think Captain Lee on the TV show *Below Deck.*) If everything goes well, by the time I become the Rose, we won't need to work, so I will put my time and passion into boating.

Embracing the Gardener and the Rose has not been perfect. I swear, once a month my wife says, "I don't want to be the Rose anymore..." Usually it is a reflection of frustrations, feelings of selfishness, and a bit of guilt. She will also frequently say that she won't need as much support in the future, but then another opportunity will come by, and she needs support (which I'm there to do). I have found that as the Gardener, sometimes I need a bit of support also, which can be a challenge to balance. All in all, it is a great system, and I'm enjoying being the Gardener now and looking forward to being the Rose in ten or so years.

How to make it work

If you have read this far into the Gardener and the Rose concept, chances are it has resonated with you in some way. In couples, one person usually knows (strongly) when the other person needs a change and needs to be the Rose. The person who needs to be the Rose tends to be a bit reluctant (which may be an understatement for some).

You need to be acutely aware of the impact of gender norms and your existing roles as a couple on the choice to embrace the Gardener and the Rose. I personally believe that classical gender roles should have no impact, but I was amazed by the number of people who were absolutely floored by the idea that I (the husband) would move 1,200 miles for my wife's career. We also moved to the Deep South, so I have quite a few stories about bias, gender norms, and more, but you need to be aware of how unspoken norms impact you. Also, if as a couple you have had a set of roles for a while (i.e., one of you supporting the other), it may take quite the push to change those roles and be comfortable with it.

I have had couples ask me if it is possible to mix the roles (i.e., one person is 75% Gardener, 25% Rose, and the other is flipped). It may be possible, but it is a question of compromise and settling. The point is that the Rose gets to take off in whatever direction they need, which will allow them to achieve more. Mixed roles mean mixed results. I'm not going to say it is impossible, but you may be able to achieve more by having clear roles and a scheduled time to switch.

Some questions to ask as you and your partner consider this concept:

What would you do as the Rose?

How long do you want to be the Rose? Also, does it matter who goes first?

What type of support do you need?

What are our boundaries? Are there any limits, like can we move anywhere?

How will we celebrate success?

How do we make sure neither of us gets burned out? How do we reconnect and support each other?

The Gardener and the Rose is not perfect. But it does provide a framework for discussion, which is the key. You can feel free to adapt it any way you want, as long as everyone is clear on their role, responsibilities, and goals. It will end up as an ongoing discussion, so don't worry about getting it "perfect"—just keep working on it.

DIVING DEEPER: For more, visit https://childfreewealth.com/65.

5

FINANCIAL PLANNING AS A GROUP

What is your long-term care plan?

"Golden Girls House."

—LUCY, FORTY-TWO, SINGLE

Financial planning as a group, meaning that it involves more than two people (friends or romantic, it doesn't change much financially), is a lot like planning as an unmarried couple. So much so that I encourage you to read the chapter on financial planning as a couple as well (page 51) if you haven't already. The challenge with planning as a group is that the number of potential financial plans goes up exponentially, as does the need for communication.

Just as with couples, groups have three options for financial planning, but with a twist:

Everything combined (one plan): With a group of three-plus, it is going to be super challenging to get everyone to agree on a combined plan. But if you can, there is a lot of power in planning together.

Everything separate (three or more plans): The roommate planning system works with a group as long as there is a good plan for splitting bills. With a group, there may be more opportunity to successfully have an individual plan for each of you yet still work together in other ways. For example, you might be a mutual support network for each other without combining finances. Support could be in day-to-day chores, or by being each other's power of attorney (POA).

Hybrid planning (four or more plans): In a group, it is possible to have a shared plan for housing yet individual plans for the rest. It is also possible to have other areas where planning together works, even if it is with small subsections of the group. Keep in mind that if there are three people in a group, there is the potential to have six financial plans. Each person you add increases the number of plans in a factorial approach. The reason for this is that while you could have one shared plan for the entire group and then four individual plans, it is also possible for subgroups to have shared plans, leading into a complex combination of individual and shared plans.

If it sounds complicated, it is because it can be. As far as I know, none of the financial planning software packages can handle group financial planning. The process for financial planning as a group must include a lot of communication and flexibility, and keep in mind that you are essentially creating a process that does not exist in the literature. When looking for help, be sure to ask any CERTIFIED FINANCIAL PLANNER™ not only about how your planning is different because you are Childfree or Childless but also about their approach to working with groups. Many CFP® professionals may not be familiar with either issue.

THE GOLDEN GIRLS OPTION

I get asked regularly about setting up a Golden Girls group financial plan. For those unfamiliar, *The Golden Girls* TV show was about four older women—three roommates, who later became good friends, and one of their mothers—living together. I often hear about people wanting to set up something like this as part of their long-term care plan. I did have one client who even wanted to do a worldwide search for the best place to have a small community for Childfree and Childless women. Spoiler alert: It is very challenging to find a place that has low cost of living, high-quality healthcare, and good safety, but it can be done if you're willing to compromise a bit.

If you are going to set up a group-living situation, you need to get your paperwork in place early (see the next section). The easiest way is to establish a partnership agreement or an LLC (limited liability corporation) that owns the place you live in. Any agreement needs to discuss all the "what-ifs," specify exactly who pays for what, and establish certain ground rules. It is a silly example, but if four of you are going to live together, what temperature is the thermostat going to be set to? (My wife and I can't agree on temperature, so I can't imagine four or more people agreeing.)

In *The Golden Girls* setup, you would be working on a hybrid financial planning system. As a group, you plan together for housing and other shared costs like utilities, yet you each have your own financial plan outside of that. It works, as long as everyone maintains their own finances. What is your contingency plan if one of you gets sick or can't afford to live there anymore? What if someone wants to bring in a spouse or a pet? What if one person wants to do an improvement on the house but the rest of the group does not?

PLAN FOR THE FIVE DS

If you are doing financial planning together as a group, at all, you need to get your paperwork set. At a minimum, that includes a partnership agreement or an LLC. With any partnership, you need a plan for the five Ds: disinterest, divorce, drugs, disability, and death. The five Ds are the most common reasons why partnerships fail, and with Childfree and Childless people, I add a sixth D: diapers (what happens if someone does have a child, planned or not). You may think that these are all far-fetched, but they happen regularly, and you need an agreement that says exactly how you will handle them.

Let me give you an example. You and four of your friends buy your *Golden Girls* home together, and then one person dies. Do you now own a home with their legal heirs? Do you have a way to buy them out? Can they move in with you? Can they force a sale? Your partnership agreement needs to say exactly what happens. You can have a buy-sell agreement built in, or even take out life insurance to buy the other person out if needed, or their share can just be willed to the rest of the group.

I use the example of buying a house together as a group because it is relatively common and easy to explain. It gets a bit more difficult if as a group you are investing in things together, or owning a business together, or providing for each other's care, or partaking in any other potential group activity. There is no way I can realistically give you advice on all the permutations of group financial planning, so it's best to get professional advice from an attorney and a CERTIFIED FINANCIAL PLANNER™.

A word about wills, living wills, and powers of attorney (POAs)

If you are in a group, particularly a romantic group, you want to make sure you have all your wills, living wills, and powers of attorney (POAs) in place early on. The government and healthcare organizations are unlikely to recognize any of the group dynamics, and your paperwork will tell them who to listen to for decisions. The other benefit of getting your paperwork set is that you will have to have a discussion with the group about who is going to make what decisions, and what your wishes are. Imagine the nightmare of your group fighting over what you want done for you if you can't make decisions and haven't left any directions. It is not a pretty picture.

The bottom line is that planning for a group is possible; it just takes good communication and planning. Most financial planning software will not handle groups, but that does not mean you can skip planning. The challenge then is to set up a structure that gets the benefits of the group while protecting you as an individual. A plan will help you get there.

DIVING DEEPER: For more, visit https://childfreewealth.com/23.

6
YOUR LEGACY

What is the worst thing about being Childfree?

"Not having a legacy to leave behind, although a legacy isn't limited to having a child."

—NADIA, FORTY-NINE, DIVORCED

As part of your life plan, you may want to think about your legacy. In the interviews I completed for *Portraits of Childfree Wealth,* legacy was often discussed as making an impact. Jesse, who we met earlier, is working on a video game that allows people to explore life options and also do something that matters to him. He is hoping that his video game, blog articles, and other contributions can be his lasting impact on the world.

My focus is on helping people. My work on this book, and on Childfree Wealth® as a whole, is designed to make a lasting impact on people's lives and finances. I can't always help people, but it is amazing when I can. Yes, I get paid to help people, which is a bonus. My hope is that my legacy and impact can be in the people served, rather than a classical legacy of leaving money to the next generation.

While I do have a plan for my money after I pass, it is not my legacy. It is just a plan so that the government does not take the money or give it to someone else. You don't have to wait until you die to make an impact or leave a legacy. Here are some cool ideas I have heard from people recently that may get you thinking:

Create a scholarship in honor of a family member. You can be part of the selection committee, pick who you want to serve, and decide how you want to serve them. The bonus is you can see the results from your impact if you design the program right.

Pick a cause and be active in it. One of my favorite charities right now is Undue Medical Debt. They buy people's old medical debt and forgive it. The bonus is that debt can be bought for pennies on the dollar, so each donation gets multiplied in how much debt it forgives. My family always struggled with medical debt, so this one hits close to home.

Create a mentorship program. Whatever you are good at, someone else wants to learn. You can take an active role in teaching people, or just set up a blog or similar platform to share what you know.

Write that book. Yeah, you can guess I like this one also.

Get nieces and nephews started. Someone I worked with wants to start a fund to help their niblings (technical term for nieces and nephews, like siblings) to get started in life or get a life experience that they otherwise couldn't afford. The idea is to have a fund so that they can study abroad, take a year off, have a house down payment, or something else.

Random acts of kindness. Your legacy plan does not need to be huge. You could find someone who is struggling, give them $1,000 cash, and potentially change their life. Or just leave a giant tip for a service worker. Or give away that piano you aren't using anymore to someone who really wants to learn.

What matters to you? What impact do you want to make? Do you want to *Die With Zero* and give it all away while you live? Is leaving an impact important to you? What are you willing to invest your time and money in? What do you wish someone had done to help you? These are the kinds of questions to ask yourself when determining what kind of legacy you want to leave behind.

Your legacy can be a financial one, a life impact, a great work of art, charity work, or just fame for throwing the biggest parties ever.

It really doesn't matter what your legacy or impact is, but deciding it upfront will change your life, financial, and estate plan.

DIVING DEEPER: For more, visit https://childfreewealth.com/87.

PART II

GET YOUR FINANCES IN ORDER

7

THE BASICS

Are you happy with your life?

"In general, yes. There are ups and downs. I hope to find a better romantic partner at some point in my life, which I think would make me happier. Otherwise, I have been achieving creative, career, and financial goals, which has been exciting and fulfilling. I live in one of the most desirable places in the country by the beach and can afford it because I'm Childfree. So that's nice."

—FELICIA, THIRTY-THREE, LONG-TERM RELATIONSHIP

In the book's first section, I talked about creating a life you want to live. With your life goals in place, you need to consider financial goals. If your goal is not to pass on money to the next generation, you will need to wind down your net worth at some point. Your net worth is a scorecard that can help you see the direction you are going in. You don't want to let growing your net worth drive all of your decisions. Uncontrolled growth, just for growth's sake, is the mentality of a cancer cell. Cancer grows and replaces healthy cells until there are no remaining healthy cells. Money and net worth can be the same.

Calculating your net worth is simple. Take everything you own and subtract everything you owe. Keep in mind we are only talking about debt here, not monthly expenses. If you have no debt, it is even simpler: it is simply the total of everything you own (bank accounts, investments, retirement accounts, properties, etc.).

Money itself is neither good nor evil. What you do with your money is what matters. You want to have a plan for when your net worth should grow and at what point you want to spend it or wind it down. You can even aim for a bit of equilibrium with your net worth, but the reality is that investments fluctuate, and so will your net worth.

The hardest net worth to get to is often zero net worth. At zero net worth, you don't owe more than you own. Many Americans will never get to this point, especially if they enjoy or rely on using debt for purchases. Once you get to zero net worth, getting to $100K net worth is a bit easier, and becoming a millionaire becomes a matter of time and good behavior after that. **Just remember that your net worth does not equal your self-worth.** Unfortunately, in our culture many people seem to believe that making more or having more makes you a better person, and that is just not true.

When you die, your estate (and total net worth) passes on to your beneficiaries. When my wife and I die, our nephews get everything. If they get $10K or $100K, that is fine. If they get $1 million, we made a mistake somewhere. The mistake is that if we have a million dollars when we die, we should have given that away, spent it, or enjoyed it ourselves while living. If we have extra money, our nephews, charities, and others could use it more while we are living than at the end of our lives. If we live to eighty, our nephews will be in their late fifties and are less likely to need it then. Charities always need money now, and you get a tax break while living. The bottom line is that we are embracing a *Die With Zero* approach to life.

START WITH THE END IN MIND

Bill Perkins wrote the book *Die With Zero: Getting All You Can From Your Money and Your Life* for the general audience, but the approach is one that is common with Childfree people. The book is about maximizing your life and enjoying your money while you have good health. Perkins describes a triangle of life consisting of time, money, and health. When you are young, you may have health but probably have less time and money. In your elder years, you may have money and time but may have worse health. It is a good concept to consider. While Perkins talks a lot about having kids and caring for them (there is a whole chapter on kids), it is still a good read for Childfree and Permanently Childless people.

Ask yourself this question: Do I care how much money I have when I die?

I've asked a version of this question to every Childfree person I've worked with, and the vast majority of them don't care about passing on generational wealth or how much money they have when they die. While they don't want their money to just go to the government, their goals are not to amass a large estate to pass on. They also don't want to run out of money while they are alive. Ideally, they would like to die clutching their last $100.

You can still give money to the people, organizations, and places that matter to you; it just might not be upon your death. If you are charitably inclined, you can donate while living, see the impact, and maybe even get a tax break. If you want to change the life of your family members, you can do that when they really need it. If you want to invest in yourself and your experiences, that is also okay.

The challenge is that a large percentage of financial education and advice is built upon the concept that you want your net worth to constantly go up. You will see this concept talked about as "protecting your nest egg" or, more technically, "conserving your principal." The concept is so pervasive that most investment advisory firms are built around the concept. Firms charge an assets under management (AUM) fee (usually around 1%) and plan on that amount going up year over year. It creates a conflict of interest when people want to die with zero, and their planner wants to keep it growing to get a bigger fee. (Side note: This is part of the reason why I don't do percentage-based investment management for my clients, and you may want to look for an advice-only or flat-fee CERTIFIED FINANCIAL PLANNER™.)

So, if you don't want to pass down generational wealth, you need to follow a different life and financial plan. Much of this book has this as a built-in assumption. I've done this because it is a commonality within the Childfree community. If it doesn't fit you exactly, that is okay. Just use what fits.

In order to truly die with zero, you would need to know when you will die and what your long-term care expenses will be. Without a good crystal ball, that is impossible. To protect yourself and get as close to dying with zero, which we call "winding down your wealth," you need a you need a safety net that includes doing the following:

1. **Have a plan for long-term care.** Either set aside money for long-term care in a separate account or have a long-term care insurance policy.
2. **Put off claiming Social Security until seventy years old.** This way you will have a guaranteed income in your later years (assuming Social Security will still be around, but that is a much bigger topic beyond your control).
3. **Set aside a cash cushion.** Just in case Social Security isn't there (or is cut back), you may want to set aside some cash and/or investments for your last years.

With those three things in mind, it becomes a task of bending the net worth curve so that it looks more like a bell curve. At some point, you need to start spending money rather than saving. That does not mean you need to buy a fleet of Ferraris (but you might); it means investing in you and what brings you joy. Here is your chance to Marie Kondo your life—spend money on things you enjoy and get rid of things you don't. Maybe you need a career change, or want to start that small business, or go back to school, or whatever... The bottom line is that you have more flexibility in your life choices and don't need to constantly grow your net worth. You will eventually come to a point where each dollar you add to your net worth is not improving you or your happiness, and therefore, you just need to stop earning and start spending and giving.

Spending money can be a challenge when you have been good at scrimping and saving, and you may end up with what I call "the blueberry problem." I've heard from multiple people that they buy frozen blueberries because they are cheaper than fresh ones. While they are right that they can save a dollar or two, when you decide you want to die with zero, just buy fresh blueberries. They're better. Set a budget, follow it, and enjoy your life.

DIVING DEEPER: For more, visit https://childfreewealth.com/88

TELL YOUR MONEY WHAT TO DO

Very few people enjoy budgeting, but we all need to do it. A budget is simply a way of telling our money what we want it to do. A budget tells us what we can and cannot spend money on. It does not need to be fancy, but we need a budget and a plan for our money.

Budgets are like diets: not every diet works for every person. I still struggle with weight, but following a low-carb diet works for me. A low-carb diet may not work for you, and that is okay. There are many budgets and budget apps out there, and they all work. The challenge is to find one that works **for you.** Here are some popular budgets and apps for you to explore:

50/30/20: In the 50/30/20 budget, your goal is to split your money into three categories: 50% goes to your needs, 30% to your wants, and 20% to your savings and debt. The 50/30/20 budget may work in an ideal world, but if you have high debt or high housing costs, it may be impossible to follow.

Cash Stuffing/Envelope Method: The envelope method is a tried-and-true budgeting system where you put cash for each spending category in an envelope at the beginning of the month. When the envelope is empty, you need to stop spending. It is simple and it works. The envelope method saw a revival recently as people started talking about cash stuffing on TikTok and other social media.

EveryDollar: This is the Ramsey tool for budgeting. It is easy to use, but there is a fee for account aggregation in the app. It is an automated way of creating a zero-based budget, which gives every dollar a job.

YNAB: YNAB (You Need a Budget) is a favorite of budgeting nerds. I'm not calling anyone out here, but if you really want great features and budgeting to the last penny, YNAB is great. I have seen couples use it, as it allows both members to be part of it.

All of these budgets are some version of a zero-based budget. In a zero-based budget, you have a plan for all your money before the month starts. The apps have different features and range from no-tech (envelope method) to minimal tech (apps). There are literally hundreds of budgeting apps out there, so don't take any of these as the only option. Just pick one you like and stick with it. I've used Mint.com forever, and I'm just too lazy to try any other apps for my personal budgeting. It wasn't until Mint.com closed that I had to change. There may be others that are better, but it is about what works for you and what you will actually use.

DIVING DEEPER: For more, visit https://childfreewealth.com/5.

MUSTS, SHOULDS, COULDS, AND WON'TS

With my clients, I use a system called the Money Management System (MMS). I created the MMS based upon a time management system that breaks things into Musts, Shoulds, Coulds, and Won'ts. (You can download a google sheet version of the system here: https://childfreewealth.com/mmsdoc.) What I like about the system is that it makes you take a hard look at your finances and prioritize your spending. It goes beyond wants versus needs.

How to use the Money Management System

Step 1: Add up all your income for the month. Remember, if you get paid weekly or biweekly, you may have some months with an extra paycheck, or a bonus, so start with what you expect to earn for the month.

Step 2: Take 10% off the top for safety and security. Our grandparents always kept a rainy-day fund. Until you have a fully funded emergency fund, this puts safety and security first. If you have consumer debt (everything but your house), the safety and security fund goes there.

Step 3: Pay for your Musts. Musts represent everything you need to stay alive, keep a roof over your head, or are required to pay by law.

Step 4: Pay for your Shoulds. Shoulds include things like paying down debt, so if you have debt, you will not have money left over for Coulds.

Step 5: Pay for your Coulds, which is discretionary spending. Coulds include pocket money and money saved for your goals. You get to choose if you spend your money on dining out or save it for that dream trip.

Step 6: Make a list of your Won'ts, which are those things we need to cut out. Won'ts are technically not part of your budget, but having a list of problem areas to watch out for and not to spend money on can be helpful.

MUSTS

In order for the system to work, you need to draw a strict line between your Musts, Shoulds, and Coulds. Here are a couple examples to get you thinking:

Groceries are a Must, as you need to eat. Dining out is a Could.

Basic transportation is a Must, but only if you drive to work. If you work from home and are part of a couple, the second car may be a Should, or even a Could, rather than a Must.

I Must take my wife out for our anniversary, while I Should take my mom out for lunch. (Sorry, Mom!)

MUSTS INCLUDE:

Housing (rent or mortgage)

Home or renters' insurance

Property taxes

Healthcare costs (if not included in your paycheck)

Utilities (gas/oil, electric, water/sewer)

Transportation (auto loan, insurance, gas, maintenance)

Credit cards—MINIMUM PAYMENTS ONLY

Any other loans—MINIMUM PAYMENTS ONLY

Any court-ordered payments (or similar)

The list of Musts is intentionally very limited. Think of it this way: What bills would you have to pay to not be on the street? Or, what are the bills you would have to pay no matter what, even if you lost your job? (My wife and I have a bit of a disagreement about Musts... She believes that caring for our pets is a Must, while I think it is a Should. When I gave her the test of whether she would pay for their food and vet bills or be on the street, she told me in no uncertain terms that I would be on the street before the dog and cat would. I hope she is joking, but in our budget, pets are now listed as a Must.)

Internet access and cell phones are common areas that people I work with list as Musts. If you work from home and need the internet to get your paycheck, okay, it is a Must. If you use the internet purely for entertainment, it is a Should.

Take a minute and add up all your Musts. If your Musts equal more than your take-home pay, something needs to change immediately. The only answer is to either make more money or lower the costs of your Musts.

Whatever money you have left over after paying for your Musts rolls over into the Shoulds category.

SHOULDS

Shoulds include things like paying for insurance, sinking funds, paying down debt, saving for an emergency fund, and more. Shoulds are almost as important as Musts. If you receive a bonus or other unplanned money, it will increase your Shoulds budget and needs to be spent in this category before you move to Coulds and spend it on whatever fun thing you want.

SHOULDS INCLUDE:

Paying off debt

Saving for your emergency fund

Internet access (unless you work from home and it is necessary for your job)

Subscriptions to streaming services/cable (pick one or two streaming subscriptions please, not all of them)

Cell phone

Disability insurance

Life insurance (only if it is needed)

Sinking funds for auto repairs, home repairs, gifts

Other Shoulds

The challenge with budgeting for Shoulds is making sure that Coulds don't sneak in. You Should be paying off your debt before you go out to dinner. You Should be paying for disability insurance before paying for a trip. If you get hurt on that trip and can't work, you will be out of luck if you do not have disability insurance.

The problem most people run into with Shoulds is that paying down your debt or saving for an emergency fund is at the top of the list. Effectively, if you are working on building up your emergency fund and paying down debt, then you will not have money left over for Coulds. Does that mean that if you are in debt, you can't go out to eat or travel? Yup. I know that is harsh, but this is exactly why we are setting priorities for your money. I'm not saying you can never have fun, but fun comes after you pay for all your Shoulds.

More about sinking funds

The Shoulds category includes sinking funds for auto, home, and gifts (I would also include a sinking fund for vet care if my wife would allow it). In a sinking fund, you put a set amount aside each month to account for big purchases in the future. Ideally your car doesn't need big repairs each month, so this is a way to save up for when it does. When you haven't been budgeting, or you live paycheck to paycheck, the idea of a sinking fund may be odd.

Figuring out exactly how much to put in a sinking fund is a bit of trial and error. For homes, the general rule is that you will spend 1% of your home's value each year on maintenance. The challenge is that there are some years where you may have little or no maintenance, while there will be other years where you will spend more than 1%. I recently had to replace the roof on my house, which was about 4.4% of the value of the house. Good thing I had a plan for it.

For your car maintenance it may be a bit harder to figure out exactly how much to put in your sinking fund. There are averages out there that say that you will spend between $750 and $1,000 each year on car maintenance, but it varies widely. If you have a newer car you are going to spend less than on an old car that is falling apart. Look at how much you spent last year as a guide.

When you haven't had a sinking fund in place, you may have what is called deferred maintenance of your car and house. You may not have had the money to get regular oil changes or change the tires. When you defer maintenance, it is put off until it is an emergency. Emergencies almost always cost more than proper maintenance, and by nature there is no way to schedule them. Once you catch up on your deferred maintenance, you may be able to lower your sinking funds.

The gift sinking fund is there because we know holidays and birthdays will come at the same time each year. My goal is for you to set a budget for gifts, not just go with the flow or buy whatever hits you at the time. Gifting is a particularly dangerous area in many people's budgets. I worked with someone who is a disabled veteran on Social Security. He came to me because he wanted to know if he should take out a home equity loan to repair his property. We worked up his budget, and he should have been able to pay for the fence without a problem. In the end, I figured out that he had "friends" and family coming by with their hands out each month the day after he got his check. He would give them money for any variety of reasons (many sounded like tall tales to me) and he would be left struggling to make it through the month. The moral of the story is, don't give money to friends and family, and set a budget for gifts.

Keep your sinking funds in a high-yield savings account. There are savings accounts now, at banks such as Ally, that offer "buckets" or a similar system to categorize your savings. You can have a different bucket for your emergency fund and each of your sinking funds, all in the same savings account. The other option is to just have a separate account for each, which may work better for some people.

COULDS

Whatever money you have left after you pay for your Musts and Shoulds becomes part of your Coulds. Your Coulds become a combination of your goals and fun money. With couples, I like to set aside pocket money for each person to spend however they want. You get to choose if you want to set aside money for dining out, traveling, saving for a home or retirement, or whatever. You get to choose your goals and the speed to get there.

Your life plan will determine where you spend your Coulds. Personally, I tend to have a debate between spending my money on things to enjoy now versus saving for the future. If you are following the Financial Independence, Retire Early (FIRE) lifestyle, you save as much as you can now so that you can retire earlier. If you are following FILE, it is about getting the right balance. I'm not great at my own personal balance. I recently debated (heavily) getting a boat now versus saving for the future. I can't afford my dream boat now, but if I put away more now, I can get my dream boat earlier. On the other hand, I can buy a perfectly nice boat now and enjoy it in the meantime, which is what I decided to do.

Buying a boat is a terrible financial decision. I know that. The bottom line is that you can do whatever you want with your Coulds. I'm not going to judge you, and no one should, as long as you pay for your Musts and Shoulds first.

WON'TS

The Won't category isn't really a monthly budget but more a reminder of danger areas to stay away from. Personally, my wife's and my danger areas are Amazon and meals out. I live in a very rural area, and it takes more than two days to get things from Amazon. The challenge is that when an Amazon box shows up at my house, I don't always know what is in it. If I don't know what is in it, I probably didn't really need it. And that is a problem.

Dining out needs a special callout. If you are still building up your emergency fund or paying down debt, dining out (or ordering in) is super dangerous. I've seen couples run up thousands of dollars in dining out each month. That is not an exaggeration. Add up how much you have spent on dining out or DoorDash, and you may quickly add it to your Won'ts.

You know what you need to cut out. If you don't, then look at your annual spending summary for your debit or credit cards. Watch out for relatively small charges that add up to a lot. For example, I've seen people spending hundreds (and even thousands) monthly on in-app purchases, especially games. I love gaming, but I have a hard-and-fast rule not to pay to play with in-app purchases. It is intentionally addictive and dangerous. I'm currently playing a game on my phone (which shall remain nameless) with a group of friends, and we had a group chat discussion about in-app purchases. I have purchased nothing, and I'm lagging behind my team. I now understand why. The top spender was spending $600 to $1,000 PER WEEK in game purchases! This definitely needs to be added to the Won't list.

DIVING DEEPER: For more, visit https://childfreewealth.com/8.

BUDGETING AS A COUPLE

Budgeting as a couple requires constant communication and a slightly different set of tips and tricks. Your budgeting system as a couple is going to depend on whether you have chosen to combine finances or not. If you have decided you are each on your own, then your role to each other is as an accountability partner. If, on the other hand, you have decided to combine some, or all, of your expenses, you have a different set of considerations. Keep in mind that it is less about whether you have a joint bank account and more about whether you are on the same financial plan (or hybrid plan).

Yours, mine, and ours

When my wife and I first got married, the advice I got was to do a yours, mine, and ours setup (a hybrid financial plan). In this approach, you each have your own account for whatever you want, and then joint expenses come out of the joint account. In principle, it seems simple and fair. In practice, the three accounts can be a challenge to manage.

In most cases, you will have different incomes as a couple. If it is a small difference (+/- 10% or less) then you may just want to ignore the difference. The issue comes when you have someone making considerably more money than their spouse. In that case, you need to choose if you are going to split things proportionally or by a flat amount. For example, we could each put $1,000 per month into the joint account or each put in 25% of our salary.

My preference is to each put in the same percentage of take-home income. While a flat percentage will mean that one person is putting in more dollars out of each check, the commitment to the joint account is the same proportionally. Depending on how much of your expenses and goals are joint, you may end up putting most or very little of your paycheck into the joint account. For example, if the only joint expenditure is for housing, then it should be less than one-third of your take-home pay.

In a yours, mine, and ours approach, the bonus is that what is not in the joint account can be spent however you want. If as a couple you have different spending habits, having three accounts may be a saving grace for your relationship. The challenge to this system is that you end up with three sets of goals or plans, which may have mixed results. If one of you wants to save and invest, while the other wants to spend, you can end up with much bigger inequities, and possibly one of you retiring well before the other.

A note on prenups, property, taxes, and the three-account method: If you are going to do a prenuptial agreement, you need to maintain separate accounts and tracking. In particular, this becomes an issue if one of you receives an inheritance. Be sure to keep any inheritance in a separate account, and not commingle it with joint funds. Also, be sure to check with your state's rules on property and titling. In community property states, all property during marriage is considered to be split evenly, even if you both put in different amount. Additionally, once you are married, you need to file your taxes as married, even if you file as Married Filing Separately. If one of you makes considerably more than the other, you may both end up paying more in taxes as you are pushed into higher brackets.

Part of the reason why my wife and I abandoned this method is that we started embracing the Gardener and the Rose. If you are embracing this approach, the point is that we are all in this together, working on the same goals and financial plan, even if each of us has different roles. If you can manage the three accounts well, it can provide a great framework, but what happens when one of you needs support or loses their job?

Everything together

The other option for couples, and the one my wife and I follow now, is to combine everything. Everyone's money goes into the same pot and is used for expenses, goals, savings, and more. The challenge with doing everything together is that you need to discuss your budget, spending, and goals to make sure they are aligned. When you have your budget meetings, the key is that both people need to be part of it, even if only one of you actually pays the bills.

While my wife and I combine everything, we are not great at discussing everything together. It is probably no surprise that my wife has delegated all the financial decisions to me. She is an epidemiologist and spends her days working with numbers and statistics, but she leaves the financial math to me. I regularly try to review things with her, but beyond smiles and nods, I don't get much feedback. It works for us, as neither of us has wild spending habits (although some may argue that my boat is a wild spending habit), but it could easily go sideways. It is not fair to delegate everything to one person in the couple, and it is something we need to work on.

In order to prevent issues, I encourage people with joint accounts and budgeting to set up an individual spending money line item (pocket money). My wife and I each have our own fun money. She spends hers on fruit dresses (dresses with fruit or vegetable patterns on them), and mine goes to the boat. It is not always equal in our case, but it works out in the end. The point is to allow each person to have some freedom with their money, within a combined budget. I don't love calling this an allowance, as that has other connotations, but if that works for you, you can think of it that way.

Keep in mind that even if you are doing everything together, your retirement accounts will stay separate. You can have a joint brokerage account, but you each have your own IRAs, 401(k)s, and other similar retirement accounts. Because my wife works in academia, she has access to both a 403(b) and a 457, which means she can put away more than I can with just my 401(k). That is fine by us, but in reality, it means she may end up with more in retirement accounts than I have. The tax benefits are worth it to us, even if it is not equal.

BUDGET TIPS AND TRICKS

This section is a bit of a hodgepodge of tips and tricks to keep you on your budget. The tips are in no particular order, as what works for one person may not work for someone else. Pick the tips that best address your issues. Remember that with budgeting, it is not about getting it right; it's about making improvements each month.

Budget meetings

It does not matter if you are a soloist or part of a couple or group; you need to schedule a weekly budget meeting. Weekly budget meetings are a chance to look at your projected versus actual spending. By looking at your budget weekly, you can make small adjustments to put yourself back on track. If you look at your budget only once a month, there is no chance to make course corrections before it's too late.

For soloists, you may want to enlist an accountability partner for your budget meetings. You both can provide accountability for each other. Accountability includes making sure the meetings happen and that you address any issues you find.

For couples and groups, make it a date night. I know there are more fun things to do than budgeting on a date night, but you need to make it a priority. It tends to be best if you set the same day each week, with a backup day in case of scheduling issues.

DIVING DEEPER: For more, visit https://childfreewealth.com/6.

Prepaid debit cards

Prepaid debit cards can help you to set a hard-and-fast limit to spending in any category. I usually recommend prepaid debit cards for online apps/purchases (think Amazon), but you can use prepaid debit cards as a technology-enhanced envelope method. Here's how it works.

At the beginning of the month you set a budget, say $100, for a category (we will say Amazon for this example). You can purchase a prepaid (and refillable) debit card online or at Walmart and put your budgeted amount on it. You remove your credit card from the app and only use the prepaid debit card. When the prepaid debit card runs out, you must stop spending. It is a rough wake-up call when you run out, but it stops mindless spending.

You can use a prepaid debit card for most categories in your budget. I've even had couples give each person a prepaid debit card for their pocket money (whatever they want to spend on). If you each have your own pocket money debit card, you can also buy each other gifts without ruining the surprise. My wife and I have joint accounts, and she knows I keep an eye on everything. She regularly uses her brother's help to buy me gifts (so I don't figure out what she's getting me), but we really should just have separate prepaid debit cards.

Don't let perfect be the enemy of good

With budgeting, your goal should be to make improvements each month. Your first month will not go perfectly, and that is okay. There will be things you didn't budget for, emergencies and life events that get in the way of the perfect budget. The reason why I suggest weekly budget meetings is that you are able to make tweaks as you go along. Make your goal to improve, not to be perfect.

Before you give up on any budget method or app, give it a run for three to six months. Chances are it is not the tool or app that is the issue, but more likely it is your own money behaviors getting in the way. It is a new skill you are building. Just like working out, it is more important to be consistent than to try to be perfect. It is not the gym's fault if you don't show up, and it is not the budget's fault if you run out of money.

Beware of budget slips and try not to make them a fall. I've seen people mess up their budget in the first week and then just write off the whole month. Don't beat yourself up; just work on making improvements next week.

DIVING DEEPER: For more, visit https://childfreewealth.com/7.

8
SET A STRONG FOUNDATION

THE EIGHT NO-BABY STEPS

What is the best thing about being Childfree?

"Childfree living truly allows you the time and freedom to explore yourself. You have the luxury of time and space to explore your past experiences as a child, as well as your experiences as an adult. You have an opportunity to truly build a life unique to you, and spend all your time cultivating hobbies, interests, and schedules that are best suited to you. I believe so many of us have grown up in imperfect households that many times leave behind lasting effects. Being that I have no other responsibilities to cultivate someone's emotional well-being, I can take that time to care for mine!"

—JOCELYN, TWENTY, MARRIED

I had a client recently call what I do "forced adulting." She's not wrong, and the reality is that we all need to grow up at some point and do the "right" things. Even my mother, who is in her seventies and says she will never grow up, needs to be an adult at some point (but that can be its own book). I do bristle a bit when people say there are "right" and "wrong" things to do, or that there are things you must or should do. It is rarely so black and white. What is right or wrong financially depends on your life and financial situation. There are some basics to help you set a strong foundation, but even those may need some tweaks to fit you perfectly. The bottom line is to set a strong foundation, but don't worry about whether you are getting it "right" or doing the "adult things."

It sounds simple, but at its most basic core, finances are about spending less than what you make and using the extra to reach your goals. When you are at the "rent-and-ramen" stage, your goal is just to make it through the month. Once you have your basic needs met, it becomes a bit more of a struggle between spending money and saving it, especially when it comes to short-term and long-term goals.

No matter what your favorite influencer on TikTok says, there is no quick path to wealth. Buying a certain product or using a specific app will not change your financial future. Also, being Childfree does not automatically make you rich. Getting to financial independence and not worrying about money takes deliberate, boring steps.

Popular financial guru Dave Ramsey has mastered helping people with his baby steps. He outlines "seven baby steps" that get people out of debt and onto a path to wealth. You need to give Ramsey credit for getting millions of people out of debt, whether you agree with him and his politics or not. The challenge is that much of his work has a religious and pronatalist bias. He assumes everyone will have children, and his baby steps reflect that. For those of us who don't have kids and aren't planning on having kids, I present the eight No-Baby Steps:

EIGHT NO-BABY STEPS FOR CHILDFREE PEOPLE

Step 1: Create a starter emergency fund to cover one month of expenses.

Step 2: Get out of debt.

Step 3: Build a three- to six-month emergency fund.

Step 4: Save and invest toward your goals.

Step 5: Get your insurance right.

Step 6: Complete estate planning.

Step 7: Plan for Mom and Dad.

Step 8: Wind down your wealth.

The point of the No-Baby Steps is to give you a framework to set a strong foundation. They are in order for a reason. There is more to finance and wealth than the No-Baby Steps, but they are the basics to living a life of Childfree Wealth.

DIVING DEEPER: For more, visit https://childfreewealth.com/127.

9

NO-BABY STEP 1

STARTER EMERGENCY FUND

Are you happy with your life?

"Overall, yes, very happy. I have zero debt, which has allowed me to work on some amazing projects that I would never have been able to otherwise. When I was younger, I saved all my summer earnings and traveled a lot in the winter. I do recognize the fact that I need to finish my master's so I can get a better job, which I've known for a long time, but I was incredibly free all through my twenties and I loved it. I know people who had kids at a very young age, and they like to say that they'll live their life after their kids leave. Honestly, I don't know if that's possible. There are a lot of things I'm very glad I did (traveling beyond dirt cheap, taking massive risks, moving all the time, minimum wage, etc.) that just wouldn't be the same in my forties, or it would be something I really wouldn't want to do at that age. I'm really glad I got to see and do those things when I was younger with practically no expenses or rent. There are a lot of things I'd never be able to do now."

—MEAGAN, THIRTY, SINGLE

My grandmother called her emergency fund a rainy-day fund. At times, her rainy-day fund consisted of cash in a coffee can, which may sound silly, but it was there when she needed it. She didn't have to worry about the bank going under or having to go to a bank teller to take money out. Remember, there was a time before ATMs, and cash at home was your own version of that.

The goal of No-Baby Step 1 is for you to build a starter emergency fund that can cover one month of your expenses (Musts/Needs only). (You need to know your expenses before this step, that is why the chapter on budgeting came first. To recap, go to page 81.) The intent is not for you to be able to rely on that emergency fund for much, but just as a small cushion to prevent you from going further into debt.

Maybe due to my grandmother's influence, I like to keep $1,000 of my emergency fund in cash in my house. There are a lot of emergencies that can be handled by $1,000 in cash. Having $1,000 is not a magic number or specific to any area, just what has worked for me. If another amount works for you, great! We have all gotten too used to using cards for everything, but you need power and the internet and/or cell phone service to use those cards. If you can keep money around without spending it, think about keeping some of your emergency fund in cash. Keep it safe, as there is risk in having cash around. I've heard of people freezing it in ice so that they stop themselves from spending it, and others who give it to their responsible spouse or friend to hide. Whatever works for you.

The rest of your emergency fund goes in a high-yield savings account (HYSA). You can google who has the best rate today, but just make sure they are Federal Deposit Insurance Corporation (FDIC) insured (this means up to $250,000 of your money is protected, or $500,000 if it's a joint account). I recommend keeping your emergency fund at a different bank than your normal accounts, so it is out of sight and you are not tempted to spend it. We don't invest our emergency funds because they already have a job, and that is to be there if or when we need it. When you invest your money, it may on average return more money than the interest in a HYSA, but you take the risk of the market being down, which can be disastrous if it is down when you have an emergency and need to pull out cash.

To get started on your emergency fund, I encourage a bit of

house cleaning. List anything you do not need for sale on Facebook Marketplace, eBay, or have a tag sale, yard sale, garage sale, or whatever you call them in your area. Chances are you have enough stuff around that you could sell to get you through No-Baby Step 1. If you don't, you may need to pick up some gig work or extra hours at work. Not having an emergency fund is an emergency in itself.

A note on gig work: The best-paying gig work tends to be jobs that other people don't want to do, or the proverbial "dirty job." I've seen people make good money cleaning houses and cars. One of my favorite small businesses is a guy who welds dumpsters. Yes, you need to know welding, but it is a great job because it doesn't have to be perfect, and it pays well because others don't want to do it or don't know how to do it. If you have a specialized skill, such as welding, chances are you will make more doing that as your side gig. If you don't have a skill, you may actually make more money working part time at a retail store than driving for Uber or relying on another generic skill.

Side note: If you have a bunch of new stuff (tags still on it) around, just return it. Even if you get store credit, you may be able to sell those store cards for cash. I've had people return thousands of dollars of stuff and check off No-Baby Step 1. The key is to build your starter emergency fund ASAP and then move on to paying off your debt.

DIVING DEEPER: For more, visit https://childfreewealth.com/128.

10

NO-BABY STEP 2

GET OUT OF DEBT

Why did you decide to be Childfree?

"My husband and I share many reasons for choosing a Childfree life. One is independence—both personal and financial. We have goals of being at zero debt by forty; this would not be possible with children."

—CLARISSA, THIRTY-FOUR, MARRIED

Debt allows you to steal from your future for purchases today. It can make you feel like you have more money or that something is cheaper. Buying a $40,000 car sounds expensive, but a $400-a-month lease sounds reasonable. The car company makes more on the lease and knows you are willing to spend more in total if you are paying in monthly installments. The hard part is that companies know how to use financial psychology against you, and they do that with debt and attractive offers.

Marketers have even gotten us to think about good versus bad debt. "Good debt" (according to marketers) includes mortgages, student loans, and debt used for investments. I don't buy that. Debt is debt. Debt means you owe someone else money. Marketing it as good or bad debt doesn't change that. Just ask the millions of people with student loan debt if it is "good" to have.

Getting out of debt is much harder than getting into debt. You can incur hundreds of thousands of dollars of debt with nothing more than your signature. With online mortgages, loans, and credit cards, you may not even have to physically sign up to pick up a bunch of debt. On the other hand, getting out of debt requires you to have a plan, set goals, and work hard.

THREE STEPS FOR GETTING OUT OF DEBT

If you are like most people and already have thousands of dollars in debt, it is time to make getting out of debt (and staying out) a priority. Here are three steps to getting out of debt:

1. Lock all your credit cards and stop taking on more debt.
2. Set a goal and make a budget to get out of debt.
3. Pay off your debt, smallest to largest.

Looks simple enough, right? It may look easy on paper, but in real life it is a challenge.

Lock all your credit cards and stop taking out more debt

It is very hard (nearly impossible) to get out of debt if you are still spending and taking on more debt. It is like filling a bucket with a hole in it.

Locking your credit cards is the first step. With many credit cards, you can easily do this in their app. Locking does not mean you are closing the card; it means you are stopping it from being used. It will stop both you and others from using it. It will stop any recurring charges (subscription fees) from being paid, and you won't be able to use it for new purchases.

It is usually at this point that people start freaking out. I've heard all versions of "But if I lock my cards, how will I pay my bills?" and "But what about the credit card points?" The whole point of locking your cards is to get you to start thinking differently. You can use cash and prepaid debit cards to pay your bills. If you are carrying a balance on your credit cards, then the points or cash back is way too expensive, and you need to ignore these features.

In addition to locking your credit cards, you need to stop taking out any new debt. The point is to break the debt cycle. If you are currently taking out payday loans, it can be difficult to break the cycle. You may need to work more or take on a side gig or part-time job to make it through.

Set a goal and budget to get out of debt

Many people try getting out of debt by putting what is left over at the end of the month toward their debt, but there is rarely any money left over. It doesn't work. Instead, you need to set a goal and budget to get out of debt. Here's an example:

Goal: Pay off $6,000 in debt over the next year.

Budget: Put $500 per month toward the debt.

It is that simple. If you get a bonus or extra money, that also goes to the debt, but every month you need to budget a minimum that is going toward debt. For most people, I tend to challenge them to put 50% more toward their debt than they have planned (e.g., I'd set a goal of $750/month versus $500/month in the example). Getting out of debt needs to be seen as a priority and emergency. You need to have a sense of urgency in removing the debt. Chances are whatever number you budget can be increased if you are willing to work harder at it. Each dollar extra you put toward your debt gets you out of debt quicker (and saves you money on interest).

Pay off your debt, smallest to largest

There are two popular methods for paying down your debt: the snowball method and the avalanche method. In the snowball method, you pay the minimums on all your debt and focus on paying off the smallest debt first, meaning the debt with the smallest dollar amount. In the avalanche method, you focus on the highest interest rate first. I recommend the snowball method, even though mathematically and financially the avalanche method is better.

I like the snowball method because of its behavioral and psychological benefits. You get to see your progress quicker and celebrate by cutting up cards as you pay them off. Quick wins help to keep us going. If you use the avalanche method, you may end up having to pay off a large balance first, and some people will give up before they get it paid off.

In both methods, you pay the minimums required on all your debts except the one you are focusing on. The point of the snowball method is that once you pay off one debt (credit card or whatever), you can then put that minimum toward the next debt, making a snowball. Once you get a few debts paid off, those additional amounts you would have paid on monthly minimums start to add up and speed up your progress.

DO I HAVE TO PAY OFF ALL MY DEBT FIRST?

Short answer: yes, except your mortgage (if you have one). I recommend paying off your debts before building a fully funded emergency fund because consumer debt in particular is an emergency on its own. With credit cards having 20%+ interest on average, that is an emergency. Student loans averaging 6% interest will double in size in approximately twelve years. The "rule of 72" can be used to figure out how many years it will take for your debt to double by dividing 72 by your average interest rate. You will quickly realize it has to be paid off now.

You also need to pay off your debt and have a fully funded emergency fund before you start investing. If you want to put enough into your 401(k) to get a company match and put the rest toward debt, I won't yell as long as you are going to stay at your company long enough to get the match. On average, the stock market returns 7%–10% (depending on your investment mix and time in the market). You have to pay taxes on those gains. Paying off a student loan with 6% interest will likely save you more money than you would earn, and it is risk free.

Think of paying off debt as investing in your future. Any interest you save is effectively a tax-free, risk-free return on your money. If you can go into retirement (if that is your goal) with no debt whatsoever, your monthly expenses will be relatively low. Also, once you have paid off your debt and built your emergency fund, think about how much you will have to save and invest toward your goals!

DIVING DEEPER: For more, visit https://childfreewealth.com/12.

DEBT TIPS AND TRICKS

Unfortunately, there aren't tricks to get rid of debt easily without an impact. That being said, I wanted to add an area to review common tips and tricks that people use (and to debunk many).

Just to get it out of the way, here's a note about debt consolidation loans: a debt consolidation loan may lower your overall interest rate but may cost you fees that make it not worth it. The danger is that a debt consolidation loan may feel like you are making progress, but it is more like rearranging the deck chairs on the *Titanic*—lots of activity that isn't going to help. Instead, work on these tips and tricks.

Credit card shuffle

The credit card shuffle consists of using 0% interest offers (or similar) and moving the debt from one card to the next. The problem with this system is that there is usually an upfront fee, and the promo rate may just be a teaser. Commonly, the upfront rate for transfers is 3%. What that means is that in order to take advantage of the 0% interest, you have to pay 3% upfront. Each time you move the debt, effectively the 3% rate compounds as you are paying fees on the fees. If you get caught and keep the debt beyond the promo rate, there may also be a retroactive interest charge. The bottom line is that you do end up paying interest *and* a fee!

What I have seen work is to contact your credit card company and see if there is a way to lower your rate without doing a transfer or incurring a fee. Occasionally they may have a promo to keep clients, especially if you have been paying on time. While you are at it, cash out any points you may have to pay down the debt. Keep the debt where it is and make it a priority to pay it off, not to shuffle it around.

Bankruptcy

If you have credit card debt, bankruptcy may be an option, but it comes at a cost. If you ask a bankruptcy lawyer if you should file bankruptcy, their answer will be yes, because that is how they make money. After bankruptcy, you may have your debt forgiven, as when filing for a Chapter 7 bankruptcy (but only after you liquidate your assets), or you may receive an adjusted payment plan, as when filing for a Chapter 13 bankruptcy. Your credit score will also be hit hard, and it takes seven years to get a bankruptcy off your credit report.

The challenge with a bankruptcy is that it does not change the behaviors that got you into debt in the first place. You also cannot do anything with debt owed to the IRS or student loans in bankruptcy. The only time I've recommended bankruptcy is in the case of a major life event that hopefully will not happen again (i.e., a major medical event). If you are deeply in debt and overdue on payments, you may be better off negotiating down the debt yourself rather than going bankrupt.

Debt consolidation

Watch out! There are a lot of debt consolidation companies out there. They make money by taking your money and negotiating down your debt (after they take their fees, of course). You can do the negotiation yourself, so don't pay someone else to do it. Debt consolidation loans bundle your debt together in a new loan (more debt) and can lower your interest rate, but you end up with the same amount of debt as you started with. Rather than consolidating your debt and just moving it around, focus on actually paying it off.

Debt negotiation

If you have any seriously overdue debts (think 120 days or more), you may be able to negotiate it down for less. The catch is that you need to have enough cash on hand to pay the entire amount you offer. Here's how it works:

The debt collector calls you. Offer to make a settlement in full for about one-third of the amount owed.

Get it IN WRITING that they will accept the amount as settlement in full.

Write them a check for the agreed amount and keep a copy of it with the paperwork. DO NOT give them electronic access to your account (EFT and the like), as they may withdraw more than agreed upon.

The best I've seen a client do is to negotiate a really old debt for 25% of what is owed. You may have more luck at the end of the month, as they are trying to make their numbers to get bonuses and commissions. If they refuse to negotiate, move to another debt and try that one.

You will get a hit on your credit report as you settled the debt for less than what was owed. The bonus is that the account you settled will no longer be reported as overdue, so it will work out and be less of a hit than bankruptcy.

DIVING DEEPER: For more, visit https://childfreewealth.com/15.

Healthcare debt

Healthcare debt is special, as there is a chance that the hospital (or health system) may have a financial aid or charity care office. This is particularly true in nonprofit health systems. If you have a big hospital debt, contact them and ask for financial aid or charity care. They will have you fill out a bunch of paperwork to see what you qualify for. You may get lucky, and they may have a plan you can qualify for, or another way to take care of the debt.

I've seen more than once where hospitals offered a very reasonable payment plan, as it is better for them to get some money than to write it off completely. For example, I had someone who owed a lot of money to a hospital offer to pay $20 per month. When they asked about how long they would be paying $20 per month, it was essentially forever, but to get out of paying a very large healthcare bill all at once is worth it.

Additionally, be very careful to make sure that you actually owe the amount shown on the medical bill. It is common practice for healthcare organizations to send you a bill before your insurance company has paid anything on it. The bill looks like you owe a large amount, and many people pay it. Wait until the insurance has made their payment and adjustment. You can also contact your insurance company if you think they did not cover it appropriately. I recently had my primary care doctor bill me almost $200 for a blood draw. My insurance company paid nothing. I found out it was coded wrong, and after they updated it, I owed $5. It was a pain to figure out, but worth it.

Other people's debt

If a loved one passes, don't be surprised if bill collectors contact you and say you owe them. Debt does not pass after death unless you have cosigned for the loan or are married and assumed the debt together. Your loved one's estate may be responsible for the debt, but not you. It is just a case of debt collectors trying to take advantage of your loss.

Also, NEVER, NEVER, NEVER co-sign for someone else's debt. If someone needs a co-signer, that means the bank has already determined that they are a bad credit risk. I don't care how much you love your friend or family member, don't co-sign for their loan. If you really need to help them, you can give them a gift of money (if you can afford it), but don't put yourself in the position to take on someone else's debt.

DIVING DEEPER: For more, visit https://childfreewealth.com/129.

STUDENT LOANS

If you have had or currently have a student loan, or if you've been paying any attention at all to politics and the news, you know that student loans are a huge issue. The problem with writing about student loans is that they are a moving target. I'm going to share some basic concepts to consider, but be sure to see what the current rules and regulations are and if they have shifted since I wrote this (2024).

Currently, there are very few ways to get your loans forgiven outside of your being permanently disabled or dying. I know that is super depressing. Bankruptcy doesn't work, and forgiveness programs have their own challenges and requirements. If you are disabled (or become disabled), be sure to apply for student loan discharge. Your loan should be automatically discharged if you are collecting Social Security Disability Insurance (SSDI), but often this requires more paperwork.

Forgiveness

The government and political pundits have been talking about student loan forgiveness since the 1970s. The bottom line is that while it is a great political talking point, I wouldn't count on it. In 2023, the U.S. Supreme Court knocked down President Joe Biden's student loan forgiveness program. The program was slated to give $10K in forgiveness per person for federal student loans and was bumped up to $20K if you had ever received a Pell Grant. I doubt this will be the last attempt at forgiveness. If we do, great! But don't count on it or make it part of your plan.

Public Service Loan Forgiveness (PSLF)

One path to student loan forgiveness that works (sometimes) is the Public Service Loan Forgiveness (PSLF) program. If you work for a nonprofit or governmental agency, you may qualify for the PSLF program. You need to work in those sectors full time (thirty-plus hours/week) and make 120 payments (ten years of monthly payments) before the loan is forgiven. The challenge is that forgiveness is a political hot button, with some presidential administrations approving fewer than 1% of applications, while others approve most applications. It is possible that you may qualify, make your 120 payments, and then not get forgiveness in the future due to political whims.

If you are on the PSLF program, you want to also be enrolled in an income-driven or income-based repayment program to keep your payment as low as possible. If you are married, you may also want to consider filing your taxes as Married Filing Separately, as it may lower your discretionary income (therefore lowering your payment).

The good thing about the PSLF program is that the forgiveness at the end is tax free (this is not the case for other programs). Just make sure you are going to commit to ten years of public service. If you think you may change careers, this option may not be good for you.

If you work in healthcare, you may also want to see if you qualify for National Health Service Corps (NHSC) programs. The NHSC program is for specific careers in specific areas (high-need, rural, and the like) and may give you a grant to pay off your loans in return for a two-year commitment. It won't fit everyone, but if it does fit you, it is a better option than PSLF.

Income-Driven Repayment (IDR)

There are a variety of income-driven and income-based payment options for student loans. The normal student loan payment is based on paying off the loan over ten years. In an income-driven program, your payment is based upon your discretionary income and type of loan. I'm intentionally not talking about specific numbers here, as they change year over year. At the end of twenty or twenty-five years, your student loan is forgiven. The one thing to watch out for is that based on current tax law, you will get a tax bill on that forgiveness.

The trick with IDR plans is that your payment will go up as your income goes up. There are a few tools to keep your income down without forgoing your pay raises. You may want to consider contributing to a traditional 401(k) or individual retirement accounts (IRA), as that will lower your income. The same goes for contributing to your health savings account (HAS) if you have one. If you are married, you may also be able to file your taxes as Married Filing Separately, and some programs will accept the lower income of you alone, not as a couple.

Refinancing Options

Most people end up with a variety of student loans and interest rates, as they get a new one each year they are in school. Depending on when you got your loans and current interest rates, refinancing may be an option. Just keep in mind that loan forgiveness applies only to federal loans. If you move to a private loan when you refinance, you may lose future options. Also, if you are married or in a couple, make sure you do not put the other person's name on the refinanced loans.

Just paying it off

In the end, all the income-driven and forgiveness programs may not actually help you. In that case, just treat the student loan like any other debt and pay it off. If you have multiple loans, pay the smallest one first so that you can see some progress. You don't want to be messing with your student loans while you are trying to live the Financial Independence, Live Early (FILE) lifestyle or, even worse, during retirement.

11

NO-BABY STEP 3

BUILD A THREE- TO SIX-MONTH EMERGENCY FUND

What is the best thing about being Childfree?

"The freedom and the amount of money saved."

—ERIC, FORTY-EIGHT, MARRIED

With your debt gone, the next step is to build an emergency fund of three to six months of your expenses. As opposed to your starter fund covering one month of your expenses from No-Baby Step 1, this is a fully funded emergency fund that we are just adding to that high-yield savings account (HYSA).

So, how do you know how many months you need in your emergency fund?

The first test is to look at your job. You need to know how stable both your job and your income are. For example, I run my own company, where my income is not guaranteed each month, so if it were just me, I would need a six-month emergency fund. My wife is a professor, so she could get away with three months because she has a much more stable job. What do we actually have? A six-month emergency fund. I tend to be a bit more cautious and want to be ready for any emergency, so we went with six months. It isn't for any scientific reason or financial calculation, just what I feel comfortable with.

The second test is a combination of what you feel comfortable with and how lucky you are. I hate to say that luck is real or should be considered, but you know if you are lucky or not. I'll ask clients if they are lucky by nature and either get a laugh (they are not) or an agreement that things tend to go their way. People who have had a run of bad luck tend to want a six-month emergency fund, and that's fine. If having six months of expenses saved makes you feel better, go for it.

On the other hand, having twelve months of expenses saved away in an emergency fund is too much in most cases. If you have a highly variable income (commissioned, seasonal, or the like), you may want to have a separate savings account for expenses during lean months. Additionally, if you are retired, you may have a cash fund to pay your bills across the year, but in both cases these are not emergency funds.

If you have more than six months of expenses in your emergency fund, then you need to invest it toward your goals. My grandmother's coffee can did not keep up with inflation, and neither will your HYSA. In order to make progress, you need to take the time to learn about investing and then invest your money.

DIVING DEEPER: For more, visit https://childfreewealth.com/130.

12

NO-BABY STEP 4

SAVE AND INVEST TOWARD YOUR GOALS

What do you want your retirement to look like?

"I want to be able to travel with my spouse without financial worry. I want to go all over the world, and I especially want to travel to all the Disney locations. I want to be able to make donations to our community regularly and without worry. I want to be completely debt free and have enough investments and retirement money to maintain a lifestyle where we don't have to worry about whether the bills can still get paid and do what we want."

—DANIELLE, TWENTY-NINE, MARRIED

Once you have your debt paid off and a fully funded emergency fund, the next step is to save and invest toward your goals. When it comes to saving and investing, you need to follow this general rule: **Invest only in things you understand.** That means you understand:

WHAT you are investing in (stocks, bonds, ETFs, etc.)

WHERE you need to hold that investment (taxable brokerage account, tax-advantaged retirement accounts, and more)

HOW it impacts your financial plan (risk/reward and achieving your goals)

Investing does not need to be complex or sexy. My goal is for your finances and investments to be boring, so your life can be amazing. I'm going to attempt to give you the core components of investing so that you can make an educated decision about your investments. This section is not intended to be all encompassing, but it should give you enough to think through your investing plan and set up a simple, passive investment strategy. If you need more help, I encourage you to reach out to an advice-only or flat-fee, fee-only CERTIFIED FINANCIAL PLANNER™. Here are a few books that will allow you to dig in deeper:

The Simple Path to Wealth by J. L. Collins
The Little Book of Common Sense Investing by John C. Bogle
A Random Walk Down Wall Street by Burton G. Malkiel

The three books are listed in order of complexity, with each one allowing you to dig in deeper. They each had an impact on me and my philosophy on investing. You will see common themes through each of them and this book. The bottom line for all of them is that simple, passive investing works and can be all you need.

DIVING DEEPER: For more, visit https://childfreewealth.com/131.

WHAT TO INVEST IN

You have endless options for investments. If you feel so inclined, you can invest in the stock market, cryptocurrencies, artwork, racehorses, commodities, real estate, private equity, and a wide variety of other things. The key is to invest only in things you understand. I'm not going to try to explain everything you can invest in, but I will look at the major buckets and forms of investing and saving. Each investment could be its own book, so please excuse my brevity and realize you can dive in as deep as you want through other books and resources.

Certificates of deposit (CDs), savings accounts, money markets, and other cash products

Most people are familiar with simple savings accounts, including high-yield savings accounts (HYSAs), certificates of deposit (CDs), money market accounts, and other cash products. When you are first starting out with saving and investing, these are a good place to hold your money. The bottom line is you are giving your cash to a bank, and they pay you back interest, though each type of account is different. CDs lock up your money for a specific period of time and guarantee an interest rate. Savings accounts and money market accounts are more fluid and have variable interest rates and are more flexible about when you take out money. Don't expect CDs or savings accounts to beat inflation, as they won't, and your purchasing power will go down over time if everything is in your savings account.

DIVING DEEPER: For more, visit https://childfreewealth.com/25.

Stocks

When you buy a stock, you buy a small part of a company. Publicly traded companies may have millions of shares, and you can buy one or more shares. The bonus of owning stocks is that you benefit from the growth of the company (capital appreciation) and may get a share of the company's profits (dividends). While there are a lot of ways to calculate a company's value, stock prices are not always directly related to the company's profit or dividend. Some companies, often called "growth companies," get a premium on their stock price because of the speed of growth and the hope for future profits.

Most stocks that you will be purchasing are publicly traded. That means that they can be bought and sold on the stock exchange, and they are regulated by the Securities and Exchange Commission (SEC). It is possible to buy stocks in private companies, but that comes with a different set of concerns. You can also buy stocks in international companies. Publicly traded international stocks are traded on their own exchanges and regulated by their local laws, not the SEC.

The first way you make money from stocks is capital appreciation. That is a fancy way of saying that the stock price goes up. If you buy one share of a stock at $10 and it goes up to $15, you made a $5 profit per share. Capital gains is at a lower tax rate than regular income and we all want to save money on taxes. If you hold that stock for a year and a day in a taxable brokerage account, you can sell it and pay the lower capital gains rate. If you sell it earlier, you will have to pay income tax.

The second way you make money from stocks is if they pay out a dividend, but not all stocks do this. Dividends can be taxed as either income or capital gains (depending on if they are qualified dividends or not), so be aware. Stocks that have a high dividend yield may not have as much growth in capital appreciation. It becomes a bit of a yin-yang problem to find stocks you like that have a balance between the price going up and paying dividends.

How you pick a stock is up to you. Anyone who believes they are smarter than the market and thinks they can pick winning stocks is soon proven wrong. It seems like almost every year, there is a stock-picking contest between the top stock pickers and a chicken, monkey, or thrown darts. You would be absolutely amazed how often the chicken, monkey, and darts beat the best and brightest minds in the financial industry.

If you pick just one stock and put all your money into it, it is like going to the casino, walking up to the roulette table, and putting it all on 00. If it hits, you make a lot of money. If not, you may lose it all. In today's world, I'm scared to invest in any single stock, especially if one tweet can cause it to soar or fall. I don't recommend that anyone invest in single stocks. Instead, I encourage people to invest in ETFs or mutual funds, which are baskets of a lot of stocks and represent a diversified portfolio.

In full disclosure, I keep about 10% of my portfolio for gambling, allowing me to pick some stocks and play with them. I don't consider this part of my investing plan. If that 10% goes to zero, it won't change my life. If it goes to the moon, then I just have more to spend on boating. The bottom line is that if you are going to pick individual stocks, do it with a small part of your portfolio, consider it gambling, and don't think you can outsmart the market.

DIVING DEEPER: For more, visit https://childfreewealth.com/26.

Bonds

Bonds effectively represent loans to companies, governments, and other groups. When you buy a bond, you buy part of a loan and expect an interest payment. You will see this interest payment called a coupon or coupon rate as bonds used to literally come with a book of coupons you can redeem for the interest payment. The interest payment is treated as income for tax purposes. Bonds are often seen as a counterbalance to stocks in your portfolio. Bonds tend to be more stable than the stock market and can help to bring down your total risk.

There are a wide variety of bonds, and each has a different level of risk. At the low end of the risk spectrum, you will find treasury bonds. Treasury bonds are guaranteed by the U.S. government and are often seen as making risk-free returns. There is some risk that the government will not pay out their bonds, but at that point we'd have much bigger issues. On the other end of the risk spectrum, you will find junk bonds. Junk bonds are offered by companies and tend to offer a higher interest rate, but with a much higher risk of default. Each bond has a rating, and you can balance the return with the risk.

Federal and municipal bonds are treated differently from a tax standpoint than corporate bonds. Federal bonds, issued by the U.S. government, are generally exempt from state and local taxes. On the other hand, municipal bonds, issued by state or local government agencies, are generally exempt from federal taxes. Corporate bonds are taxable at both the state and federal levels. Depending on your own tax situation, you may be better off buying one type of bond or another.

In 2022 and 2023, I bonds came back to popularity. I bonds are a type of savings bond that is indexed to inflation. My grandfather used to buy each of us a savings bond on our birthday, and I used mine to buy my first car. Savings bonds and I bonds can be bought directly from the U.S.

government at Treasury Direct. Each type of savings bond has its own rules and limits, so be sure to check those limits before you purchase them.

Just as with stocks, buying just one bond is not a great idea. In addition to the risk of the bond not being paid, bonds are for a certain amount of time. What may look like a good return for the next year or two might be a terrible return five years from now (especially if interest rates have gone up). To lower your risk with bonds, you can buy them in ETFs or mutual funds as a basket of bonds.

DIVING DEEPER: For more, visit https://childfreewealth.com/27.

Exchange Traded Funds (ETFs)

When you buy an exchange traded fund (ETF) you can buy just one share but get a part of a wide variety of stocks. Most ETFs are passively managed index funds. What that means is you can buy one fund, such as VTI, and effectively get a piece of just about every stock on the U.S. stock market. VTI is Vanguard's ETF that represents the entire U.S. stock market. At the time of writing (December 2024), VTI included 3,750 stocks. ETFs have a fee, which is called an "expense ratio." VTI's expense ratio is 0.03%. That means if you buy $1,000 in VTI, you will pay $0.30 in fees each year (that is very low; my goal is to keep total fees under 0.10%).

The bonus of buying an ETF is that you can find one that buys the stocks you want, or the segment you want to buy in, and buy everything at once. ETFs trade much like stocks and go up or down in value as the underlying stocks go up and down. You will also get any dividends from the stocks passed through to you. There are also ETFs that hold a bucket of bonds. By buying one ETF, you can effectively get a diversified portfolio of stocks or bonds.

John Bogle deserves credit for creating the first index funds, which later became what we know as ETFs. Bogle is also the founder of Vanguard. If you read his book, *The Little Book of Common Sense Investing*, you will see the formation of these thoughts. Many people, who call themselves Bogleheads, follow a simple three-fund portfolio such as this:

VTI: covers the U.S. stock market

VXUS: covers the international stock market (minus the United States)

BND: covers U.S. bonds

This is exactly how I recommend most people invest. More details are at the end of this section, but when you buy these three funds you end up just riding the stock market's overall performance. It is the core of a passive, long-term investment strategy, which is what I recommend for my Childfree and Permanently Childless clients.

DIVING DEEPER: For more, visit https://childfreewealth.com/28.

Mutual funds

Mutual funds and ETFs are very similar, but mutual funds can be either passively or actively managed and tend to have higher fees. Mutual funds are baskets of stocks or bonds that are picked by a fund manager. Watch out for high fees on mutual funds, as some can charge you over 1% per year. Mutual funds are nice because you can set up automatic investing and buy parts of a share. It is a good way to "set and forget" your investments.

You will find mutual funds in your 401(k) accounts, as the fees for the funds help to defray the cost of the 401(k)s and simplify investing. Each 401(k) has its own chosen funds, and you will be limited to those funds. Look for the ones with the lowest fees. You can do a three-fund portfolio with mutual funds just as with ETFs:

VTSAX: covers the U.S. stock market (it invests in the same thing as VTI)

VTIAX: covers the international stock market (does not include the United States, same investments as VXUS)

VBTLX: covers U.S. bonds (invests in the same thing as BND)

If you don't have access to Vanguard mutual funds, chances are there are similar ones from other companies. You may also find mutual funds that cover the S&P 500 or similar indexes, and they provide a wide range of stocks to invest in.

Be careful not to buy mutual funds in taxable accounts. Actively managed mutual funds adjust their investments regularly, and this may result in a hefty tax bill for you. Effectively, they are selling one stock to buy the other, and you have to pay taxes on the gain.

Target date funds

A target date fund (TDF) is a special type of mutual fund that is very popular in 401(k) accounts. You may also see them called target retirement funds (TRFs). These funds have a mix of stocks and bonds that shift as you get closer to retirement. Effectively, they start out completely in stocks, and they increase the amount of bonds they hold as the years go by. You can buy a TDF for a set time (e.g., ending in 2050). TDFs have a slightly higher fee, as they are mutual funds, but they tend to be reasonable. For example, the VFIFX, Vanguard's 2050 target retirement fund, has an expense ratio of 0.08%.

Vanguard's TDF just buys a mix of Vanguard funds, so it is similar to a three-fund portfolio, but with less work for you. If you have a low-fee TDF as an option and don't want to think more about your investments, it is fine to just pick one that fits your time scale. If you want to be a bit more aggressive (take on more risk in the hope of more gain), pick a date further out. If you want to have a less aggressive portfolio (more bonds), pick a closer date. The three-fund portfolio is a bit better, but not enough for most people to make a difference.

DIVING DEEPER: For more, visit https://childfreewealth.com/38.

Alternative investments

There's a giant list of alternative investments out there. You can invest in just about anything you want, but I'm not going to recommend any of them. I don't recommend alternative investments because even after studying them, I don't completely understand each of them, and I don't see a reason to change from a simple three-fund portfolio. Someone is going to read this and be mad at me that I did not include their favorite alternative investment as a recommendation, and that is okay. It is also okay if you want to dive into understanding other investments and build them into your financial plan.

I do want to call out cryptocurrencies. There is a lot of potential in blockchain technology, and crypto may have a place in our future. How cryptos perform over time is still to be determined. I spend a considerable amount of time trying to learn about cryptocurrencies, and I still feel like a novice. I will share that many of the crypto experts recommend putting 1% of your portfolio in crypto. With a 1% allocation it doesn't matter if it goes to zero, and if it goes to the moon, you still have a piece. I'm okay with this conceptually, but I haven't bought any crypto directly in my portfolio so far. Keep in mind that by buying all of the U.S. stock market, you are indirectly investing in crypto, so that could be enough.

DIVING DEEPER: For more, visit https://childfreewealth.com/30.

Real estate and real estate investment trusts (REITs)

While it may seem odd to see real estate in the same list as stocks and bonds, remember that real estate is just another option to invest in. Many people gravitate to buying real estate, as they feel like they understand it.

The concept is simple: buy a property, rent it out, and make sure the rent covers the mortgage. The problem is that, in most cases, you are taking out debt to make these investments. You can guess that I'm not in favor of this practice. I wouldn't recommend margin loans (investing in the stock market with debt), and I'm not going to recommend buying investment property with debt. If you want to buy it with cash, that is a different story.

The other problem I have with real estate investing is that it may not match your Childfree lifestyle. If you are a bit more nomadic, or are likely to move to another area, buying real estate can lead to issues. While some will argue that you can pay a company to manage your property, my argument is that if you are going to pay a management company, you might as well buy a real estate investment trust (REIT).

With REITs, you can buy into real estate managed by others and get a share of the profits. REITs are required to pay out 90% of their net income to investors, and you can buy REITs in a wide variety of properties. You can find REITs that specialize in residential housing, commercial real estate, self-storage facilities, healthcare, and more. Then again, 4% of VTI is invested in REITs, so you may not even need to buy separate REITs if you are following the three-fund portfolio approach.

Keep in mind that the property you buy to live in is often different from the one you would buy to invest in.

WHERE TO HOLD INVESTMENTS

Once you know what you want to invest in, the next step is to know where to hold that investment. Sometimes, the type of account where you hold the investment will determine what you can invest in, so it is a bit of a chicken and egg decision. Where you hold your investments is a relationship between your goals and tax planning.

A quick overview of tax issues (more detail later in the book): I'm going to super-simplify taxes and tax planning. My goal is to give you just enough to think through your options, but while investing can be simple, tax planning can be very complex.

In the United States, you are taxed on your worldwide earnings. You don't get a choice to pay taxes or not. You do get a choice in when to pay your taxes and sometimes in what taxes you pay. Here are the basic taxes you need to understand in order to invest:

Income tax: This tends to be the highest overall rate. You pay income tax on what you earn at work but also on investment income, which includes interest and some dividends.

Short-term capital gains: If you hold an investment for less than a year, it is a short-term gain or loss. It can offset other capital gains or losses; otherwise it gets taxed like income.

Long-term capital gains: If you hold something for a year and a day, you can have the more favorable long-term capital gains (LTCG) treatment. Many people pay 15% LTCG, but there is also a 0% and 20% bracket.

Our tax code is long, confusing, and challenging even for tax professionals. The bottom line for you is to understand when you are paying tax on your investments and what type of tax you are paying. For example, you usually want to keep your income-producing investments in your tax-advantaged accounts so they don't drive up your income tax. That means your bonds go in retirement accounts (which are tax advantaged) and stocks can go in either retirement or brokerage (taxable) accounts.

Tax advantaged vs. taxable accounts

Your retirement accounts, health savings accounts (HSAs), and deferred compensation accounts are considered tax-advantaged accounts. "Tax-advantaged" means they have tax benefits (if done right) and therefore you need a plan for which account to use, and when. There are two common forms you will see: a traditional account and a Roth account.

Traditional account (pre-tax): In a traditional account, you get a tax break when you put the money in, it grows tax free, but you pay taxes on what you take out.

Roth account (post-tax): In a Roth account, you pay taxes before you put it in, but it grows tax free and comes out tax free.

Which tax-advantaged account you use depends on your own tax situation and financial plan. The core question is, would you rather pay taxes on the seed (what you put in) or the harvest (what you get out)? I tend to favor Roth accounts, which taxes the seed. That is because I believe taxes are going to keep going up over time. If, on the other hand, you think your taxes will be less in the future, you may want to use a traditional account.

One bonus of using traditional accounts is that it lowers your gross income. This can be very helpful for those in income-driven payment plans for student loans and for qualifying for other governmental programs such as healthcare subsidies. If you need to lower your gross income for any reason, go with traditional. If not, you may want to go with Roth.

The other reason I like using Roth accounts for retirement is that traditional accounts have required minimum distributions (RMDs). Depending on when you were born, somewhere between age seventy-two and seventy-five, you must take RMDs from your traditional accounts. This includes 401(k)s and IRAs. For many people, RMDs may force you to take out so much money that it puts you into a higher tax bracket, and there is no way around it. Roth accounts do not have RMDs. There are other benefits to Roth accounts, such allowing you to get access to your contributions before being fifty-nine and a half, but that is for the advanced planning section.

HSAs are a special type of tax-advantaged account. HSAs have a rare triple tax benefit—you get a tax break when you put money in, it grows tax free, and it comes out tax free when used for medical expenses. The downside is you must have a high-deductible health plan (HDHP) to have an HSA account, and there are limits to how much you can contribute. Many HSAs can be invested just like any retirement account, and you can carry the balance over each year.

DIVING DEEPER: For more, visit https://childfreewealth.com/70.

An account that is not tax advantaged is considered a taxable account. Brokerage accounts are an example of a taxable account, as are savings accounts and CDs. In taxable accounts, you pay taxes (income or capital gains) as you realize the gain (i.e., when you take the money out). In general, fill your tax-advantaged accounts first, then your taxable accounts.

401(k)s, 403(b)s, and other random numbers and letters

For most people, a 401(k) or 403(b) is the biggest opportunity to save in a tax-advantaged retirement account. While there are small differences, for employees 401(k) and 403(b) accounts seem much the same. The biggest difference is that a 401(k) is offered by a for-profit company, while a 403(b) can be offered only by nonprofit organizations and some governmental organizations. If you work for the federal government, you may have access to a TSP (thrift savings plan) in place of a 401(k). (Trivia point: the numbers—401(k), 403(b), etc.—have to do with where they are located in the IRS code.)

With a 401(k) or 403(b), you put your money in and can withdraw it penalty free at age fifty-nine and a half. If you take the money out before then, you have to pay a 10% penalty. There are some ways to get access to your account earlier, but those should be considered only with the help of a CFP® professional and a CPA.

Employers have an option to make a 401(k) or 403(b) match. With a match, you put in a certain amount of money, and they match it. For example, it is common to see that an employer will match 50% of your contributions up to 6% (e.g., you put in 6%, and they will put in 3%). Be sure to check to see how long before the match vests, meaning how long before the company match is yours to keep. You will always be able to keep your own contribution, but it is common for employers to vest their match after three years. That means if you are with the company for fewer than three years, you will be forgoing your match.

Most employers are now offering both traditional and Roth 401(k)s or 403(b)s. The bonus of this is that you can put up to the 401(k) max ($23,000 in 2024) in either Roth or traditional, and there is no income cap. This is different from a Roth IRA, which has an income cap. Most employers put their matching contributions in the traditional side (so they can get a tax break). If you put your contributions into the Roth side, they will still match it, just as traditional. Once you hit fifty years old, you are able to add an additional catch-up contribution ($7,500 in 2024), and 403(b)s have allowed an additional contribution ($3,000 in 2024) for employees who have been with the company for fifteen years.

The good thing about 401(k) and 403(b) plans is that you can automate everything. You can set a percentage or flat amount to contribute each paycheck, and it will automatically invest in the mutual funds you have selected. Once you are out of debt and have an emergency fund, you should start with contributing 15% of your paycheck to your 401(k). Fifteen percent isn't a magic number; it is just a place to start that works for many. You should keep increasing your contribution until you max out your 401(k). A good trick is to try to put at least half of any raise toward your 401(k). For example, if you get a 4% raise, increase your 401(k) contribution by 2%. Keep in mind that the employee contribution max is across all your employers, so if you have more than one job, be careful.

If you are self-employed or have any 1099 income, you can set up a Solo or Individual 401(k). With a Solo 401(k), you can effectively contribute as both employee and employer. The exact amount you can contribute is based on your net income for the business, but if you have enough income, you could contribute up to $69,000 in 2024. Also, since you are setting it up yourself, you get to pick where it is and what funds you invest in (mine is at Vanguard).

A special note about thrift savings plans (TSPs): TSPs have a few quirks, but overall they are a very low-cost program. They offer lifecycle funds, which work very similarly to target date funds, and you can combine the C fund (S&P 500) with the I fund (International) and G fund (Governmental bonds) if you want something similar to the three-fund portfolio.

When you leave an employer, you may want to consider doing a direct transfer rollover of your 401(k) to your new employer or to an IRA. The key is both to keep your fees down and not lose old 401(k) funds. I've had to spend months helping clients find old 401(k)s, so do yourself a favor and consider rolling them over immediately to keep everything clean.

DIVING DEEPER: For more, visit https://childfreewealth.com/32.

457(b) and deferred compensation programs

I want to call out 457(b) programs and other deferred compensation programs as a special option. You will only find 457(b) programs in nonprofit and governmental organizations. The bonus of a 457(b) program is that you can get access to the money when you quit (or retire) no matter what age. If you have an option of a 403(b) and a 457(b), I'd put enough in the 403(b) to get the match, and then max out the 457(b). If you have access to both, you can contribute a maximum of $23,000 (in 2024) to each, as they are treated as separate plans.

Pensions

Pensions are dying off but still exist in some governmental and union environments. When they are offered, usually there is an option for another plan to opt out of the pension. The other program may be a 403(b) or similar. Before you sign up for a pension or the alternative, take a good look at the requirements. Many pensions require ten-plus years of service, and if there is any question of whether you will be in the job in ten years, pick the alternative.

A pension effectively buys an annuity to give you a fixed income in the future. The nice part is that you have a guaranteed income, but the downside is you don't have much control. If you have a 403(b), you get to pick the investments and when you take your money out, which can have a huge tax impact. The one pension I do recommend is if they offer lifetime health insurance with the pension. In that case, the combo of a guaranteed income and healthcare is a winner.

When you go to cash out your pension, they may give you an option to take a lump sum instead of payments. This is a good time to reach out to a CFP® professional to look at the pros and cons. It isn't a cut-and-dried choice, so you want help, as you can't change your mind later.

DIVING DEEPER: For more, visit https://childfreewealth.com/55.

Individual retirement accounts (IRAs)

Individual retirement accounts (IRAs) allow you to save up to $7,000 (in 2024) annually toward your retirement, either in a traditional or Roth IRA. You can also contribute an extra $1,000 (in 2024) if you are over fifty years old. IRAs are rather simple, but there are some income limits you need to keep in mind.

For traditional IRAs, you are able to deduct your full contribution if your employer (or your spouse's employer) does not offer a 401(k) or similar retirement plan. If your employer does offer a 401(k), then there are income limits to deducting a traditional IRA. Even if you are above the limit, you can still contribute to your IRA, but it is a non-deductible contribution. A non-deductible contribution can then be rolled into a Roth IRA—you may have heard of this as a "backdoor Roth"—but be careful, as there are rules (called "pro rata rules") that you have to consider if your traditional IRA has both deductible and non-deductible contributions (seek professional advice from a CFP® and/or a CPA).

For Roth IRAs, there is an income limit. As your income goes up, the amount you can contribute to a Roth IRA goes down until it phases out completely. You may still be able to make a backdoor Roth contribution, but at times that may be more hassle than it is worth. I've seen too many people mess up this process to be able to recommend it more universally.

Remember that your IRA is just an account. Once your money is in your IRA, you then have to invest it. All too often I will find that people have been contributing to their IRAs for years and then complain that it is not going up (or down). This is because their IRA is still sitting in cash. IRAs allow a lot of flexibility in investment options, but you need to actually buy the ETFs to have them invested. If you have any doubt, go check your existing IRA and see if it is invested.

You can have your IRA at any brokerage or custodian you like. The rule to follow is to go with the one with the lowest fees and that you like. I tend to encourage people to put all of their accounts at one custodian for simplicity. My personal preference is Vanguard (more about that in the next section).

Brokerage accounts

A brokerage account is also called a "taxable account." It is as simple as it comes. You put money into it, buy investments, and pay taxes on any gains. You can put in as much money as you want and take it out at any time. There are times where the flexibility of a brokerage account can beat the tax benefits of a retirement account, especially if you are going to retire early or need the money before age fifty-nine and a half.

You can pick any broker or custodian you like. They all have their ups and downs. I recommend using Vanguard. Vanguard is special in that the people who own their funds own Vanguard. They don't have shareholders who need to make money off the brokerage, so their fees tend to be some of the lowest. One downside is that their technology and overall support are bare-bones, and that turns some people off. Personally, I don't need my broker to be fancy, have the best tech, or throw confetti in an app when I buy a stock. If you do, then just make sure their fees are low.

A note on robo-advisors, AI, and assets under management (AUM) fees. If you are going to follow the simple three-fund portfolio I recommend, then you don't need to pay for a robo-advisor, AI, or an AUM fee. All these services charge you a percentage of your assets, each year, for life. If you need help investing, you can work with an advice-only or flat-fee CERTIFIED FINANCIAL PLANNER™ and pay them on an hourly or retainer basis to get things set up and make adjustments. Don't pay ongoing fees for fancy tech or help if you don't need it.

DIVING DEEPER: For more, visit https://childfreewealth.com/36.

Bank accounts

At some point, we have all had some type of bank account, and you probably understand the basics. Once again, the key is to keep your fees low (for checking accounts) and interest high. You are likely to get a higher interest rate from online banks, as they often fight about who has the best rate each month and don't have to pay for a brick-and-mortar building. Just make sure they are FDIC insured.

In 2023, we saw some big banks collapse, and the FDIC came in to protect the deposits. The FDIC insures your cash at banks up to $250,000 per person, per bank (this limit rises to $500,000 if it is a joint account). If you have more than $250K in cash in the bank, my first question is: Why? In the event you are looking to make a big purchase, then split it between banks to make sure it is not over the limit.

HOW INVESTMENTS IMPACT YOUR FINANCIAL PLAN

Once you know what you want to invest in and where to keep it, the next step is to make sure that you understand how your investments impact your financial plan. At its most basic, this is a balance between risk and reward. If you take on more risk, you may get to your goal faster, but you may also have a bad run of years and it could take longer.

The stock market returns 7%–10% per year, on average. That average is based on decades of data, and a mix of stocks and bonds. The exact percentage doesn't matter as much as your understanding that on a year-over-year basis there may be wild swings. To show how this works in practice, let's look at the last ten years for VTI:

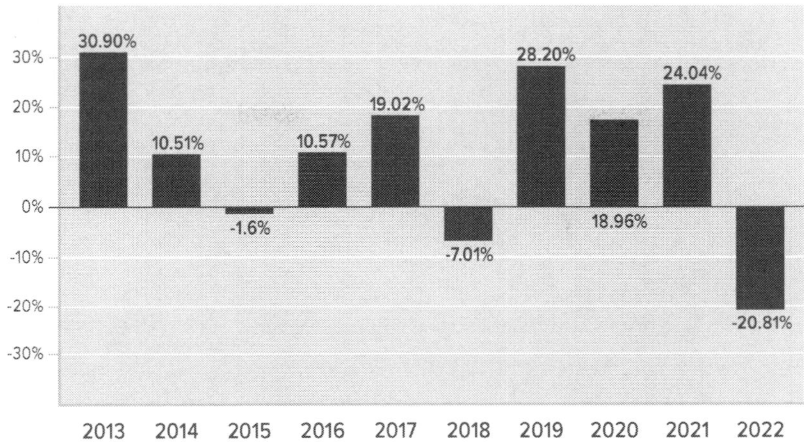

The result for the last ten years for VTI was an 11.64% annual return, but it varied from a 20.81% loss to a 30.90% gain (this is only in share price; dividends are added on separately). If you can hold on for the ride, and not pull out your investments, then you can put 100% into stock and do what J. L. Collins has made popular: VTSAX and chill. If this rollercoaster is going to make you sick, then you need to balance things out with some bonds.

There are a bunch of rules of thumb, such as that your bond allocation should be equal to your age. I don't buy that. There are assessments, such as the one we use at Childfree Wealth®, that use your willingness to take risk to make a recommended allocation between stocks and bonds. Any assessment is a place to start. Here are some basic guidelines that may help:

PORTFOLIO COMPOSITION OPTIONS:

100% stock: if you are able to set it and forget it, you are betting on the market going up over time. This is great for people who are young and able to take on risk. Young is not an absolute number, but think about it as the first half of your life. As you get older, and need to live off the stock, you may need some bonds to balance it out.

60% stock/40% bonds: The classic balance for retirees. The challenge is that you may not get enough growth to make up for inflation.

Somewhere in between: If you want to try to find a Goldilocks point with a mix of stocks and bonds, go for it. Each time you increase your bond allocation, your risk tends to go down and so does your return. If your investments are keeping you up at night, either you don't understand them or have taken on too much risk.

Investment goals

Your investment goals will also shift how you invest your money. If you are looking to embrace FIRE and retire as early as possible, you are likely to take on more risk (that is the VTSAX and chill approach). If you are looking to just maintain your wealth, you might take on less risk.

If you are looking to die with zero, I've seen people both invest 100% in stock and in a less risky 60/40 portfolio, as there are two schools of thought. The people investing 100% in stock are trying to get the biggest return and aren't worried if their portfolio goes down, since they don't care what is left at the end. The 60/40 people are more Zen about it and are okay with their current wealth, as they just want to slowly run it down. They don't take chances because they aren't taking their money with them to the grave.

Lately I've found myself relying more on the client's comfort level for setting their portfolio than anything else. What can be interesting for a couple is when one person is a risk taker and the other is not. Use your own judgment, and the goal should be to get your investments to a place where you set them and forget them.

Rebalancing

If you have read other financial books, or talked to a financial advisor, they will often talk about rebalancing. The idea is that if you pick a 70/30 portfolio (or whatever numbers work for you) and it gets out of whack (say 75/25), you rebalance and sell some of your stock and move it into bonds. This can be considered active rebalancing. The challenge is that when you rebalance, there are costs (often hidden in the bid-ask spread) and potential tax consequences in taxable accounts. The bid-ask spread is the difference between what you pay for the stock and what it was sold for. It may only be pennies, but they add up.

Rather than worrying much about actively rebalancing, I follow a passive approach. If your mix is not where you want it, just adjust it with your new purchases and sales (i.e., buy more bonds or stocks with your next contribution). It won't be exact, but it saves you fees and hassle. Simple, passive, long-term investing works. As John Bogle says, "Don't just do something, stand there!" We only make changes to our investment mix if an underlying fact changed (such as your life had a major change, and your goals are different now).

DIVING DEEPER: For more, visit https://childfreewealth.com/37.

Three-fund portfolio

For most people, I recommend a simple three-fund portfolio. It is the core to simple, passive, long-term investing. Here's how it works.

First, pick your mix of stocks and bonds. Then you put 80% of your stock allocation into VTI (U.S. stocks) and 20% into VXUS (international stocks); any remaining percentage goes into BND (U.S. bonds). Why 20% in international stocks? International stocks are a good counterbalance for any wild market swings in the United States and allow us to have a piece of both developing and developed countries across the world. The result is three funds: U.S. stocks, international stocks, and bonds. If you are putting 100% into stock, you won't have anything in your bond allocation. Here are two examples:

100% STOCK PORTFOLIO:

VTI: 80%
VXUS: 20%

60/40 STOCK/BOND PORTFOLIO:

VTI: 48%
VXUS: 12%
BND: 40%

You buy those ETFs, then set it and forget it. If you have a mix of tax-advantaged and taxable accounts, put the bonds in the tax-advantaged account. Each time you buy in or sell to get money out, you can adjust the percentages for passive rebalancing.

When your friends ask if you are invested in a particular stock, you can say yes. You have bought them all. If someone says they have a hot tip, ignore them, but know you already have that stock in your portfolio. It is a boring but effective way to invest.

DIVING DEEPER: For more, visit https://childfreewealth.com/39.

DIVIDEND REINVESTMENT PLANS (DRIP)

A quick note on dividend reinvestment plans (DRIPs). When you buy your ETFs, you will have an option to reinvest your dividends. As long as you don't need the money, go ahead and check yes. What that means is that as you get dividends from the ETF, it will buy more of the ETF. Set it and forget it. If it is in your taxable account you will have to pay taxes on the dividends, but it is a good way to keep investing more.

A SPECIAL WORD ABOUT ESG INVESTING

There is a spin on the three-fund portfolio that I want to mention, as it is how I invest personally. Instead of investing in VTI, VXUS, and BND, I invest in ESGV, VSGX, and VCEB. These funds are Vanguard's ESG version of the total stock market. ESG investing looks at the company's impact on environmental, social, and governance factors.[6]

6 "ESG Investing," Vanguard, accessed November 16, 2023, https://investor.vanguard.com/investment-products/esg.

There are many ways to do ESG investing, but Vanguard's approach is an opt-out list. ESGV invests in approximately 1,500 companies, fewer than half of the ones that VTI invests in. The 1,500 in the fund meet the ESG requirements that Vanguard has chosen. For example, ESGV does not invest in fossil fuels. The challenge is that you may be passing up some returns by not investing in fossil fuels or other companies on the "naughty list." ESG funds also have a higher expense ratio (ESGV is 0.09%), as they have to do additional work to maintain ESG funds.

If you dive deep into ESG investing, you are going to find there are a wide variety of options. You will find actively managed funds that have an opt-in list rather than opt-out. In these funds, they actively pick stocks to invest in, use their proxy votes to improve companies, and advocate for specific values. You can also find "anti-ESG" funds, such as DRLL, which only invests in U.S. energy and fossil fuels.

If you want to spend the time, you may be able to find a fund that coincides with your values. The challenge is that if you get too granular, you may end up with a portfolio that isn't really diversified, or a realization that all companies have some bad stuff in them.

I've gone down the ESG rabbit hole and came back to investing in Vanguard's ESG funds. It is not perfect, but I want my money to go toward things I believe in (and not to others). It is completely up to you, but realize you may be giving up some financial gains to follow your values. I'm okay with that, and I personally believe that ESG investing is better for the world in the long run and should be better financially at some point.

Wash sales, day trading, and other fancy stuff

If you have read this far, I'm hoping you aren't buying single stocks or day trading. If you get the itch to day trade, don't. You need to be careful with frequent trades, as you can fall into an issue with the IRS wash sale rule. The rule says that if you sell a stock at a loss, and then buy it back in a certain time period (thirty-one days before or after), even in another account, then the loss is disregarded. What that means in English is that it is possible to owe more money than you made. The current highest I've seen is a tax bill of over $1 million on $200K in gain.

Also, skip any other fancy investing apps or games. Buying options (calls and puts) has become popular online, but this is gambling, not investing. If you get the urge to make a big bet on any one stock, keep in mind the risks and limit yourself.

GETTING HELP INVESTING

So, what if you read all of this on investing and still want help? That's fine! The key is for you to learn how to invest, and some people learn best with help. Here are a few considerations:

Anyone can call themselves a financial advisor. If you go to a financial advisor who sells insurance products (and makes their money off commissions), then don't be surprised if they say that insurance is the solution to all of your problems. What you are looking for is a CERTIFIED FINANCIAL PLANNER™. A CFP® professional is trained to help with comprehensive financial planning.

Only fee-only. Look for CFP® professionals who are fee-only. That means you pay them, not someone else. Fee-based CFP® professionals get paid to sell you products, so there is a conflict there. Don't get confused by fee-only and fee-based; they may sound the same, but there is a huge difference.

Avoid percentage-based AUM fees. If you are looking to die with zero, then someone charging you a 1% AUM fee has a conflict of interest, as they want your net worth (and their paycheck) to steadily go up, and that is not what you want.

Make sure they are a fiduciary. Fiduciaries have to put your interest ahead of their own. This is really important.

Ask them how your plan is different because you are Childfree. If they give you a snarky answer like "You will change your mind," just walk out.

Use an advice-only or flat-fee financial planner. Advice-only means you pay them for their time on an hourly, project, or retainer basis. You can use them to set things up, or make changes, and then not pay on your assets for life. Childfree Wealth® is an advice-only, fee-only fiduciary and specializes in helping Childfree people. If for any reason we are not the right fit for you, there is a list of advice-only planners at Advice-Only Network.

The bottom line is to take the time now to learn how to invest. Simple, passive investing works, and you can learn how to manage your own investments (with or without help). There are times, especially when looking at tax planning, where you will want to work with a professional, but it doesn't have to be a lifetime commitment.

13

NO-BABY STEP 5

GET YOUR INSURANCE RIGHT

How do you plan to pay for long-term care?

"Should I ever require long-term care, I plan on hiring a healthcare worker from a service to either come out however many times a week is necessary, or live-in if something drastic has happened to me. My husband is okay with moving to a retirement community/old folks' home, but once we're properly planted, I want to stay independent, in my home as long as possible. We've got savings, and I'll have an inheritance from my stepmother's trust, and hopefully we'll be mortgage-free by retirement, so I don't think cost will be much of an issue at least for a while."

—MADDIE, THIRTY-TWO, MARRIED

If investing and saving are the offense in your financial plan, insurance is the defense. Childfree people have different insurance needs than parents, and many of the general financial rules don't fit us. For example, disability insurance is more important than life insurance for us. We also know we need a plan for long-term care and to know who is going to take care of us when we are older.

DIVING DEEPER: For more, visit https://childfreewealth.com/132.

LIFE INSURANCE

Just about every time I have a client ask me about life insurance, it is because someone is trying to sell it to them. There are huge commissions in selling life insurance, and don't be surprised when your family or friends try to get you to buy what they are selling.

While talking to Anna (from the *We're Not Kidding* podcast) and her husband, Grant, on my *Childfree Wealth®* podcast, we got into a discussion about disability insurance. They had gone to their local insurance broker and asked about disability insurance and walked out with half a dozen *life* insurance quotes. Even though they had asked for disability insurance and didn't even need life insurance, the broker was pushing them on life insurance because brokers make a lot more from signing up new life insurance policies.

The general rule is that you need ten to twelve times your salary in life insurance. This rule applies only if someone else is relying on your income to live in the event of your death. If you are a SINK (single income, no kids), chances are that no one is relying on your income, and you can skip life insurance. If you are DINKs (dual income, no kids), chances are that you can live on either one of your incomes, so life insurance is not a priority (unless one of you does not work).

It is going to be very rare that I'm going to suggest that a Childfree person get life insurance. The two most common times I'd recommend life insurance are if you have a considerable amount of debt (which should have been addressed in No-Baby Step 2) or if you have a business and need a life insurance policy to buy you out after you pass. Small-business life insurance planning can be a challenge, and you may want to work with a CFP® professional to look at options.

If you are going to buy life insurance, buy only term life insurance. Term life insurance is simple. You pay a premium (ideally the same one across the policy; this is called "level term life"), and if you die during the term of the insurance (ten, fifteen, twenty years or some other time period), your beneficiaries get paid. Some people use these policies to pay for burial expenses, but you are better off just setting aside money for that, as it is going to take a while for a life insurance plan to pay out. If your employer offers group life insurance for some nominal amount, like $5 a paycheck, that is fine and probably more than you need.

Don't fall for gimmicky life insurance

If you have an existing life insurance policy, you may be a bit stuck. The way to make the most of it may be a 1035 exchange to a hybrid long-term care and life insurance plan, or a long-term care/annuity combo. I don't usually recommend these policies unless you can't qualify for standard long-term care (LTC) insurance, or you are trying to get out of another life insurance product. The bonus is that you can get some LTC coverage from the cash value of your life insurance, but it is unlikely to cover the entire cost.

The bottom line of life insurance

If you have hung out on social media, chances are you have seen someone trying to sell you life insurance. They are selling some type of whole or hybrid life with a cash value. It gets repackaged as different things, and the current fad is IULs and "infinite banking." Here's the bottom line: they are selling you a spork because they make money on it. (For those who are unfamiliar, a spork is a spoon and fork combined and it does neither job well.) A hybrid life insurance plan combines insurance and investing, and the only thing it does well is pay a commission to the person who sells it.

If that wasn't clear enough: DON'T BUY GIMMICK LIFE INSURANCE.

DIVING DEEPER: For more, visit https://childfreewealth.com/72.

DISABILITY INSURANCE

As Childfree people, we can skip life insurance, but not disability insurance. If you are a SINK and become disabled, you may be sunk. Social Security Disability Insurance (SSDI) may cover you if you have a disability, but the amount is likely to be pitifully small and won't cover your expenses. For soloists, this can be a life-changing experience. Even for DINKs, you may have a second salary to rely upon, but can you live on one salary for the rest of your life with increased healthcare costs from a disability? Probably not.

The basics

At its core, disability insurance is simple. If you can't work, it covers your salary. Plans usually cover 66%–70% of your salary. The reason it doesn't cover 100% is that if you pay for it out of pocket, the benefit is tax free. It is one of the few times when you can get income (in the form of a disability payment) and not pay income taxes on it. Depending on the policy, it may pay you until you hit sixty-five, seventy, or for a certain number of years. The reason it ends at sixty-five or seventy is that then you can go on Social Security as a retiree.

If you are receiving a disability payment, chances are you will qualify for SSDI also. The challenge is that once you apply for Social Security Disability, it can take months (or years) before you are finally approved. Once you are approved, you will be paid back to the date you applied (a retroactive payment), but that doesn't help in the meantime. Also, your disability insurance policy may be lowered by any SSDI payment, so be sure to read the fine print.

Disability insurance can cover what you are trained to do (this is called an "own-occupation policy" or something similar), or it can cover any job you are able to do. The classic example of the difference is if a surgeon loses dexterity in their hands. They can no longer do surgery, but they could do other jobs. With an own-occupation policy, they would be able to put in a claim and receive benefits if they can't do surgery. Without an own-occupation policy, that surgeon is getting nothing, as they can still do other jobs, even if it means working at McDonald's. Try to get an own-occupation policy if you have any specialty training (i.e., my own disability policy is own-occupation, as financial planning is a skill I trained for).

Short-term vs. long-term

You can get both a short-term disability (STD) and long-term disability (LTD) policy. LTD usually has an elimination period of 90–180 days. Simply put, that means you don't get paid for the first 90–180 days. A short-term policy can fill in that gap. So can your emergency fund. If you have a fully funded emergency fund of six months, then covering ninety days should not be hard.

State programs

Some states are starting to make their own disability programs as a supplement to Social Security. In these programs, you pay a percentage of your income to be part of a family and medical leave program. Watch out, as some state programs use family size to determine benefit eligibility, so it is yet another place where being Childfree changes things. That being said, take whatever you can get, but in most cases I would not count it as a substitute to your own disability policy.

How to get disability insurance

Your employer may be the cheapest place for you to get disability insurance. While these programs are cheap, they tend not to be portable, so when you quit your job, it is gone. Also, if your employer pays for it, you may have to pay income tax when you start claiming benefits. To get around this, some employers will pay for the policy but make you pay taxes on it, which works out the same as if you had paid for it yourself.

If your employer does not offer disability insurance, or you are self-employed, the next place to try is whatever national organization you are part of. For example, I'm a member of the National Association of Personal Financial Advisors (NAPFA), and I get my disability insurance through their group plan. Chances are there is a national group plan that will fit your situation. It may even be worth joining a group just to get disability insurance. For example, I have had luck with people joining the Freelancers Union to get disability insurance (and their definition of freelancers is pretty broad, so it can work for many people).

The third, and most expensive, option is to go to an insurance broker. Group plans tend to be cheaper and easier, but sometimes they aren't an option, especially for self-employed people. Be sure to go to a broker you trust to quote you only disability insurance, and don't get the bait and switch like Anna and Grant did. For my clients, I use LLIS for disability quotes. I use them because they are not commission driven, and they work with financial planners like me to find the right policy without the sales pitch. Standalone disability policies vary based upon your health and employment. Some careers are more dangerous than others, and they cost more. There is also a health screening to make sure you are insurable.

If you don't have disability insurance in place yet, put down this book and get signed up. You may have to wait until open enrollment to sign up with your employer, but be sure you know when that is.

DIVING DEEPER: For more, visit https://childfreewealth.com/73.

LONG-TERM CARE INSURANCE

Who's going to take care of you when you get older? UGH! I have a love/hate thing going on with this question. I hate the question because of all the implicit bias. Someone asking the question is expecting others (their kids/grandkids) to take care of them, even if that isn't what happens a lot of the time. I love this question because it allows me to talk about long-term care planning, which is something we all need to do.

Here are the stats. The census looked at adults over fifty-five and asked if they got any financial support from their family.[7] They found that for Childless adults, 2.5% got financial support from their family. They also found that for parents, 1.5% got any financial support from their family. The bottom line is we all need a plan for long-term care, as not many of us are getting financial support. The big difference is that Childfree people know they need a plan, and this is a topic with most of my clients.

Understanding the costs

In 2022, the average cost for a year in a private room at a skilled nursing facility was $108,000. On average, men will need 2.2 years of care, and women 3.7. Do the math and you will find out that is a lot of money. Add in that long-term care costs are rising by about 5% each year, and the costs at the end of your life could literally be millions.

Now, we won't all need to be in a skilled nursing facility, and averages suck. You could be lucky and never need care, or unlucky and need decades of care in a memory facility. The problem is that if you don't plan for long-term care, you will end up in a Medicaid facility. Medicare does not pay for long-term care, and Medicaid pays only after you have spent through your assets. Medicaid care is not the best, to say the least, and not something I would recommend to any of my friends. The truth is, in the United States we do a terrible job of caring for our elderly, but that is not a surprise to most of you.

Creating a long-term care plan

The bottom line is that you need a plan for long-term care. My recommendation is to have a plan in place by your midforties. Why midforties? That seems to be the sweet spot for long-term care insurance policies. In

7 Tayelor Valerio, et al., *Childless Older Americans: 2018.*

your midforties your parents tend to still be in good health, and qualifying should be easier. Additionally, I've looked hard at long-term care insurance policies, and buying one before your midforties does not save you money, but rates tend to pop up at fifty. It isn't a perfect science, so get a quote for you and your life to make an informed decision. You can self-insure (set aside money specifically for long-term care), buy a long-term care insurance policy, rely on Medicaid, or select the opt-out-of-life option.

Before I go into insurance policies, I want to discuss the opt-out option. I frequently have clients who have chosen euthanasia or similar programs as their long-term care plan (i.e., they are opting out of life). With more states offering compassionate care and euthanasia programs in addition to things like suicide pods in Switzerland, the opt-out is becoming a real choice for many. I'm not going to debate the ethical or political issues here, but it can have a real impact on your life and financial plan. The challenge with the opt-out is that if you plan on it and don't save for long-term care, you may not be able to change your mind. The good thing about the opt-out is that it is possible to literally die with zero and pick your time to leave this world. If you are not 100% sure whether you will opt out, then plan for long-term care costs. If you plan for long-term care and change your mind, the worst case is you won't be able to claim on the insurance.

LTC insurance is expensive because long-term care is stupidly expensive. In my experience, LTC insurance is an option for people with somewhere between $500K and $3 million in net worth. If you have less than $500K, chances are you will end up on Medicaid and you should plan for that. Over $3 million, and you may want to consider self-insuring (setting aside money). The reason for this range is simply the cost of LTC insurance. If you have less than $500K net worth, there just isn't an affordable option at this time. I use the same ranges for couples as for soloists. That may not make sense at face value, but couples get a break on LTC insurance, and single women have the highest overall policy costs. The range changes if you are in a state with a long-term care income tax, but more on that later.

I recommend using standalone LTC insurance policies. These policies have one job, which is to provide for your long-term care. LTC insurance reimburses you for your expenses for care, up to a daily or monthly maximum. Unlike health insurance, which pays the bills directly, LTC insurance reimburses you. That means you get to pick your care, submit the bill, and then get paid back (as long as you meet the requirements). The result is that these policies cover in-home, assisted living, and skilled nursing facilities. You (and your family) get to pick the care you need, and they cover it.

LTC policies kick in after you have two or more problems with activities of daily living (ADLs). ADLs include bathing, eating, dressing, transferring (i.e., moving from the bed to a chair), toileting, and handling incontinence. Once you need help with two or more ADLs, you can put in a claim, but there is usually an elimination period of 90–120 days or so. (Good thing you have a fully funded emergency fund.)

You can pay for your policy monthly, annually, or in some cases with what is called a ten pay or one-time payment. If you are paying monthly or annually, your costs can go up if the insurance company gets approval from your state. Additionally, if you miss a payment, they can cancel the whole policy. For those who can afford it, you can pay the whole policy upfront or in ten annual payments. The nice thing about this option is that it locks in your premium, and you don't have to worry about missing a payment (but it is pricey). There are example policies and prices on the Childfree Wealth website at https://childfreewealth.com/blog/long-term-care-childfree. If you are paying the policy upfront, plan on spending a minimum of six figures.

While life insurance rates are based upon your health, for LTC insurance your rates can be impacted more by your parents' health. If one of your parents has dementia, Alzheimer's, or another cognitive decline diagnosis, you can expect your rate to go up considerably. If both of your parents have a cognitive decline diagnosis, chances are you will not even be able to get a quote for LTC insurance. This is part of the reason why I say forty-five is a sweet spot. The older your parents get, the more likely they are to get diagnosed with dementia or Alzheimer's.

I'm intentionally not including sample plan prices in this book, as they change too frequently. Just as with disability insurance, I use LLIS for LTC quotes. You will need some numbers to get a good quote. As of 2023, here are the numbers I use: $250 average daily benefit, two years of care for men, four for women, 3% compound interest inflation, ninety-day elimination period, and if you are a couple, a shared care rider. A rider is an add-on to an insurance policy that allows couples to "share" total years of coverage, which is nice. The U.S. average daily benefit from 2022 is $250, and it varies greatly state by state, so google what the average daily costs are in your state. Get a quote and see what it works out to for you. Note: you need to be thirty or older to get a quote, and I've yet to see someone buy a policy before forty with the exception of people getting out of a state plan, like in Washington.

If you are going to self-insure, the key is to set aside enough money to cover long-term care costs, and it needs to be invested to return more than the 5% compound rate that long-term care is increasing by. If you have enough money in your HSA, that is perfect, but few will. Keep in mind that you will also need to cover taxes if you have a brokerage or traditional account. This money also needs to be "sacred" and not used for other retirement costs.

State plans

Washington was the first state to create an income tax to cover long-term care. Other states are looking to do a similar thing. The problem is that it is crap coverage. Here's how it works in Washington (as of 2023): You pay an extra income tax of 0.58% for a minimum of ten years. In return, you get a $100 per day benefit for one year ($36,500) toward long-term care, but only if you stay in Washington. If you move, thanks for the donation.

It is probably obvious at this point that a benefit of $36,500 isn't even going to take the edge off most people's long-term care costs, especially decades from now. The reason states are doing these plans is to shore up Medicaid. Medicaid is primarily paid for by the state, and long-term care costs are very high. It isn't really about you having your long-term care covered at all.

Washington did allow people to get a private two-year long-term care policy in order to be exempt from the tax. So many people applied for LTC insurance that the companies stopped taking applications from Washington. While I gave you a net worth range earlier, if buying LTC insurance is going to save you 0.58% in income tax every year for life, it changes the equation.

Other states are putting in similar policies and likely already have since I wrote this. Just beware.

DIVING DEEPER: For more, visit https://childfreewealth.com/76.

SOME QUICK NOTES ON HEALTH INSURANCE, MEDICARE, AND MEDICAID

Don't cheap out. If you don't have healthcare through work, pick it up on the marketplace.

If you are self-employed, it is tax deductible.

If you are in a couple, make sure to check both sets of benefits each year to see if you are better off on one policy or alone.

If your health plan qualifies for an HSA, use it.

If you have a choice between a high-deductible healthcare plan (HDHP) that qualifies for an HSA, and one that has a lower deductible, I usually recommend the lower deductible.

PROPERTY, CASUALTY, AND OTHER INSURANCE

Since we are talking about insurance, we can't forget your home, car, and umbrella insurance. As your net worth goes up, so should your insurance coverage. What worked when you were young and broke no longer works when you have some money.

Auto, home, and umbrella insurance work together. You can get a $1 million umbrella policy relatively cheaply, and that is a good place to start. An umbrella policy picks up where your car and home insurance run out and covers you up to $1 million or more. If you don't have umbrella coverage, you are responsible for any loss that totals more than your car and home coverage. Your umbrella policy will have minimums that your auto and home (or rental) policies need to have. Get them to match, and you will be in a good place. My umbrella policy even works with my boat insurance. The point is to have good coverage in case of an accident or other liability. You don't want to risk your hard-earned money on someone slipping and falling.

A couple things to check out:

- For your auto insurance, see if they have a roadside assistance program. Often buying this through your auto insurance will be cheaper than AAA or another service.
- If you use your car for work, especially gig work like Uber, make sure it is covered.
- On your home or rental insurance, look for a cyber or identity theft rider. Many companies are now offering cyber coverage at a reasonable rate, and it covers a wide variety of things including identity theft, cyber bullying, and even wire fraud.
- As your net worth goes up, you can increase your umbrella policy, but when you get over $3 million to $5 million, it may not be worth it for the risk.

Additionally, you need to make sure you have the right insurance for your work. For example, I have a $1 million policy for Errors and Omissions for my financial planning work. Each profession has its own risks, and if you run a small business, you are responsible for everything.

Just like with life insurance, consider skipping gimmicky insurance. This includes things like critical illness, cancer insurance, legal insurance, alien abduction insurance, and more. Yes, there really is alien abduction insurance, but it is a gimmick. We buy insurance for things that are likely to happen, and only if we can't afford the cost of the event. If you get taken by aliens, I'm not sure you are going to be worrying about claiming on that abduction insurance.

The bottom line is to get the right insurance, at the right time, no more, no less. You can be overinsured just as much as you can be underinsured. Buy insurance on things that are likely to happen in your life that you cannot afford out of pocket.

DIVING DEEPER: For more, visit https://childfreewealth.com/74.

14

NO-BABY STEP 6

ESTATE PLANNING

What is the worst thing about being Childfree?

"It's hard to think about estate planning because I don't know who to leave it to. I have four nieces/nephews, but my husband has thirty and several great-nieces/nephews."

—JOY, FIFTY-FOUR, MARRIED

Governmental and healthcare systems fall apart when you don't have a next of kin. The only way to protect yourself is to make sure you have the right paperwork in place. You need a will, living will, healthcare directive (and medical power of attorney [POA]), financial POA, and in-case-I-die file. The paperwork itself is very simple, but the thought process behind it can take some time.

I often get a question about what age you should be when creating your estate plan. The answer is whatever age you are now. As Childfree people, we need to have this paperwork on file immediately, no matter what our age is. The paperwork will tell people who to trust in place of next of kin, which is really important for us.

DIVING DEEPER: For more, visit https://childfreewealth.com/133.

WHO DO YOU WANT TO GIVE YOUR STUFF TO?

In the United States, you can leave your stuff to just about anyone. I say just about anyone, as your married spouse has a right to any property bought together and your 401(k) unless they waive that right (and it varies by state). As a single person, it is completely up to you. You can give your money to your family, friends, charities, your pets, or to pretty much any combination you can think of. When both you and your spouse pass, it is much the same.

Wills between couples are often very simple. You each get the other person's stuff when they pass. The question you need to ask is who gets your stuff if you both pass. Also, if you are in a couple or group but not married, be sure to check the section on estate taxes. Married couples get a benefit in that there is an unlimited gift tax exemption between them, but it is not the same without the paperwork of marriage.

So, who do Childfree people leave their stuff to? Well, if you are following the wind-down-your-wealth approach, there shouldn't be much left. Yes, you may have your physical items to pass on, but those can be outlined in your will. You should be giving to friends, family, and charity during your life, when they can get more use from it. It becomes a balancing act, but intentional giving while you are living can not only improve lives but get you a tax break. But what about what is left?

Having worked with a broad spectrum of Childfree clients, I've heard a wide variety of ideas. I do feel that Childfree people are a bit more charitably inclined, and often a large portion (or all) of their estate goes to their favorite charity. I've had people give to the national parks, local tribes, animal shelters, medical causes, and more. Each choice is valid, and it is completely up to them (and you).

If you ask your family what to do with your money, they will say to give it to them (or their kids). Our personal plan is that our nephews will get whatever is left over, but our hope is that it is not much. If you decide to give money to your family, one thing you do need to decide is who is getting what percentage. In our case, we have three nephews, two from my wife's brother, and one from my sister. The question is, does each of the nephews get one-third or does it get split in half (for the two families) and then split again? We decided on the latter option, but they are both valid.

A word about pets. We have a mastiff and a cat who is a jerk. Our mastiff, Colt, is very sweet, but he is big (like 150+ pounds). Not everyone is willing to adopt a giant dog and a jerk cat. We may have to "bribe" someone to take care of them in our will. Leaving money to care for your animals is very common. Your will should state both who gets your animals and if they get any money to take care of them.

The bonus of doing a will is that it can be changed at any time. You can decide now to give your money to your family and then later change your mind and give it to your favorite charity (or vice versa). Whoever you pick to get your stuff should also be the beneficiaries on all your accounts. You can name a beneficiary on your accounts, including retirement accounts, and then it will pass outside of the will. Passing things outside of the will keeps them out of the probate process, saving time and money.

A WINDING-DOWN-YOUR-WEALTH REALITY CHECK

If you truly don't care about who gets your money after you pass and want to wind down your wealth, then you need to start making changes now. There may be a point in your career when each dollar you earn is going to your estate, which you don't care about. That means you are working when you don't have to. If you still enjoy work, and would do it for free, fine. If not, maybe it is time to retire, follow your passions, go back to school, do an encore career, or something else.

ESTATE TAXES

On December 31, 2025, the Estate and Gift Tax exemption will fall to around $6 million per person from over $12 million currently. That may sound like a lot, but if you are saving and investing (and not spending much), it is possible that you will be past this exemption when you pass if you don't manage your estate well. The U.S. government taxes estates over this exemption at a whopping 40%. That means if you are leaving money to family, and the total is over $6 million, the government is going to take nearly half of the rest. I don't know about you, but I don't want the government getting any more of my money than they already do.

You can avoid estate taxes by planning while you are alive. You can set up an annual giving plan to family, friends, and charity. In 2024, you could give $18,000 to anyone and not pay gift taxes on it. If you do that every year, you can give away a large estate and avoid the government taking 40%. Also, amounts given to 501(c)(3) charities are not subject to estate taxes, so you can just give it to them instead of the government.

Another way you can avoid estate taxes is to spend and enjoy your money while you are alive. It is your money, and you deserve to enjoy it. I probably spend just as much time, if not more, with my clients talking about spending money rather than saving it. It is often hard for people to shift their mindsets, but rather than worrying about how to avoid estate taxes, maybe you should just do more of what you enjoy. It doesn't matter what it is. Remember, no one else gets a vote in how you spend your money. If you want to blow it instead of giving it to your family, that is your prerogative.

WHO IS GOING TO MAKE DECISIONS FOR YOU?

While the choice of who to give your money to is hard, the harder choice for many is, who is going to make decisions for you if you can't? There are three roles we need to fill:

Executor of the Will: makes decisions for your estate after you pass
Medical Power of Attorney (POA): makes medical decisions for you if you cannot (i.e., if you are incapacitated)
Financial Power of Attorney (POA): makes financial decisions for you if you cannot

If you have spent any quality time on Netflix, I'm sure you have seen some of the horror movies about caregivers taking advantage of their elderly family members. Unfortunately, elder abuse is very common, and who you choose to make decisions for you is an important one. In couples, your spouse is usually the first one to make decisions for you, but what if they pass before you or you are both incapacitated? For soloists, especially if they don't have close family or friends, it can be very hard to find someone you would trust.

Let's start by looking at the minimum requirements to fill these roles: they need to be an adult and willing and able to take the role on. That's it. You wouldn't want to name a stranger because they may not be willing to take the role on. You also can't name a child, because they can't legally sign contracts or make many of the decisions that need to be made. If you don't pick someone to fill these roles, someone in the healthcare or state system will make the decisions for you, and that is a crapshoot at best.

I know, nothing I have said so far is helping you. I'm just trying to go over the thought process. The first place to start is to look at your family and friends. You want to see if you can find someone whom you would trust with your money and your life. It is common for people to pick a different person to be their medical POA than their financial POA. Each person has their own strengths and weaknesses. You also really want someone younger than you. If you pick your parents, the chances are that you will outlive them.

If you can't find someone you can trust, hire a professional.

You can pay a professional to be your trustee, executor, and POA. You may not be able to find one person to do all three, as financial services may not want to take on the medical POA, but if you look hard enough, you can find someone you can pay. You don't need a trust to enlist the services of a trustee (although they would love it if you had a trust they could manage and charge you a yearly fee). You can state in your will or POA documents that the professional is paid hourly for their work, and they can do everything for you.

Each state has its own rules about what professionals can do these tasks for you. The best place to start is either with a local estate or eldercare attorney or a local bank. Attorneys also regularly act in some of these roles and may be fine taking on the task. Local banks, which you will often see listed as a "bank and trust," used to offer these services regularly. When Grandma couldn't pay her bills, they took care of it for her. Now, local banks are dying off, but they still exist in some areas.

Make sure they are a legal trustee and fiduciary in your state. Trust companies will often be able to show you how they meet the fiduciary and trust standards, what their insurance and emergency plans are, and make you comfortable that they will execute your wishes. Companies that have "custody" of clients' investments must go through a surprise audits and meet a series of regulatory requirements.

The bonus of hiring a professional is that you know they will do what you say, and you don't have to be a burden on anyone else. The people you assign to these roles will have guidelines about what decisions to make and how to make them. There is always a bit of leeway. Professionals tend to lean toward being more conservative in their decisions, while a family member may (or may not) lean toward whatever helps them. For example, if you need expensive healthcare, a professional trustee is going to follow your wishes, while a family member may see that as their inheritance being "spent." It is your money and your life, and you want them to follow your wishes.

In full transparency, I've been working on finding a nationwide solution to this for over two years and have had limited success. In California, you can hire a professional fiduciary to serve as your POA and executor, but that works only in California. I found one attorney in Georgia who offers an "aging ally" service and other states like Texas where attorneys absolutely refuse to be a medical POA. The trust companies I have spoken to will take on trusts only with $10 million to $100 million or more and have no interest in you if you are going to wind down your wealth. Additionally, each state's trust laws impact what trust companies can and cannot do, which can complicate things.

Enter the Childfree Trust

Since I couldn't find a solution, I decided to create one: the Childfree Trust. The good news is that a solution exists; the bad news is that it isn't cheap, and my company, Childfree Wealth®, can help only so many people.

I'm going to outline what goes into the service we provide to give you an idea of what you are looking for, even if we can't help you personally.

I introduced you to Erin, my editor, and Cheddar, her lovely dog, earlier, and I'll use them as a hypothetical example here to explain what needs to be covered. Erin and Cheddar provide a unique example, as they are a bit nomadic, and their plan reflects many Childfree people. The fact that they can be in a different state each month provides unique challenges that need to be addressed by their Childfree Trust.

So, here's the problem: What happens if, heaven forbid, Erin is in a car crash and needs to be in the hospital for a week? Here are a series of questions that need to be answered, immediately:

Who makes medical decisions for her?
Who pays her bills? (both at the hospital and at home)
Who lets Cheddar out and takes them for a walk?
What happens if she needs long-term care?
Who informs her work, loved ones, etc.?

Each of these questions can be handled by having a loved one who you can count on, or you have the Childfree Trust in place to handle it. The challenge is that it all needs to be in place before it is needed, and it needs to be flexible enough that it meets the legal requirements of whichever state they are in when it occurs. Also, the in-case-I-die file needs to be updated regularly so that we know where Cheddar is and what to do.

To add on to the complexity of the example above, what if Erin is winding down her wealth and can't afford trustee services in her elder years?

I brought the above example to a pile of attorneys and trust companies. I had many literally laugh in my face at the thought of serving a client like this. I had others tell me it was impossible or not business they want. If you are going to work with an attorney or trust company to act as your POA/emergency contact, make sure they understand the complexity of your situation and are ready to handle everything. I couldn't find one, so I ended up finding a set of partners, John Steiner and Robert Allan, who have over thirty-five years of trust experience. I've joined the board of their trust company, Welon Trust, committed my own money to it, and together we can now offer a comprehensive product.

To serve Erin and the millions of other Childfree people out there, we developed a Childfree Trust product. Here's how it works:

Each client pays an annual subscription fee that covers life, financial, tax, and insurance planning in addition to estate planning and their roles as medical POA, financial POA, and executor.

We meet with the clients regularly to understand their life and financial situation, including key contacts (like where they live and who can let out their dog if there is an emergency).

The client lists Childfree Wealth® and Welon Trust as their emergency contact, and we provide emergency support 24/7.

When clients cannot care for themselves, Childfree Wealth and Welon Trust step in. We can step in for a short period of time, such as for a disability or as long as they need it.

We make a lifetime commitment to the client as long as they make the same to us. That means if they do die with zero, we will continue to be their POA and executor to make sure they are cared for.

There's a bunch of legalese, financial planning, and investment advice that comes with the Childfree Trust, but that's the basics. My wife and I were the first ones to create a Childfree Trust for ourselves, and my company is responsible for the rest of our lives and will one day bury me. It can do the same for others. In 2024 the annual subscription was $10,000. You can join the waiting list by emailing trust@childfreewealth.com or visiting the Childfree Wealth® website.

What is still keeping me up at night i s that my company can serve only a couple of thousand people, and there are millions of Childfree people out there who may need this service. Sure, I might be able to grow the company over time to handle more, but that still is less than 1% of all Childfree people in the United States (approximately 50 million adults in 2024). So, take this chapter, and bring it to your local attorney, bank, trust company, etc., and see if they are willing to help, as we need a long-term solution for millions of people. I'm happy to share my "recipe" for helping Childfree people with others in hopes that more people can be served.

DIVING DEEPER: For more, visit https://childfreewealth.com/86.

GETTING THE PAPERWORK DONE

The actual paperwork for setting up your will and POAs can be very simple. There are fill-in-the-blank forms you can use, and I regularly recommend that people use the website Trust and Will. You can fill in the blanks and then just have it witnessed or notarized based upon your state's rules and regulations. If you have a complex estate, or are using a professional trustee, or a Childfree Trust, you are going to want to enlist a local estate attorney.

In most cases, creating a will and setting beneficiaries can take care of things after you pass. Attorneys may encourage you to put everything in a trust to "protect it" and to bypass probate. Trusts can make things easier for your executor and are a requirement if you are working with a trust company, but they come at a cost to you in both time and money. Frequently I've seen people set up trusts on paper but not actually fund them or make them "live," which means they spent money on something they aren't using. If you take the time to create a trust, you need to make sure it is regularly updated and funded appropriately.

Make sure you get all your paperwork done and signed. If you go through the work of putting it in writing but don't actually sign it (in accordance with your state rules), it is just a useless piece of paper. Once it is signed, you should keep both a physical and electronic copy of all documents, and make sure the executor and POAs have the same copies.

DIVING DEEPER: For more, visit https://childfreewealth.com/81.

HEALTHCARE DIRECTIVES AND MEDICAL POAS

While each state has its own quirks, in the end you will have a healthcare directive and a medical POA, which may be together or two separate documents.

Your healthcare directives will state what you want and don't want done for your care. Such directives give medical professionals and your POA a guide. While there can be a lot of nuance and choices, here is where you state when (or if) they pull the plug on you. For example, my parents are split. My father wants every machine and heroic efforts. My mother wants none of that. It is a good thing they have it in writing. It is also a good thing that I'm my mother's POA rather than my father, as he might not follow her wishes. Make sure whoever is your medical POA will do what you ask them to do.

Once you complete your healthcare directives and medical POA, ask your primary care doctor to put it on file. Most doctors and hospital systems now have electronic medical records, and the hope is that by putting it in the system, it can easily be found in case of emergency.

FINANCIAL POA

Financial POA documents vary greatly, and once again, your state will have its own rules. Ideally, you would like your POA to be "durable" and "springing," if your state allows it. "Durable" essentially means that it is still in effect even after you are incapacitated (which is what you want). Depending on your state, they may allow a POA to be "springing," which means it comes into effect only after a date or event (e.g., when you are incapacitated). If they do not allow springing POAs, then your POA may be in effect the moment you sign it. This can work for some people, yet others may be concerned. Effectively, if you sign a POA that is not springable, it is "live" when you sign it. That means the person who you say can be your POA can act now, even if you are not disabled. If it sounds like a bunch of legalese, that is because it is, and you may want to consult an attorney for more information.

The thing to remember about a financial POA is that you get to decide both what they can and cannot do on your behalf. For example, you might want them to be able to pay your bills, but you probably don't want them to be able to change the beneficiaries on your accounts. You can also specify what your money can and cannot be used for. You need to find a balance between giving someone full control and just enough to do their job, without being cumbersome.

DIVING DEEPER: For more, visit https://childfreewealth.com/84.

IN-CASE-I-DIE FILE

An in-case-I-die file is a file (preferably a physical printed file or a secure online file) that has a list of all of your accounts, passwords, key information, and final wishes that you share with both the executor of your estate and any POAs. Since I do all the finances in our household, this file was one of the first things I built for my wife. It is also called an I-love-you file, as it takes care of your loved ones after you pass. My own personal file includes not only financial information but also things like who the plumber is and how to take care of the things I do around the house.

The best way to create one is to keep a running list of all accounts and key people you contact over a three- to six-month period. I use a longer period, as some things like property taxes come up only twice a year for many people (and may just be once a year). I have most things on auto payment, so if I do pass, most of it will be automatic, which works for many. Even though it is automatic, it needs to go on the list so that your loved ones don't worry about it.

No one really wants to talk about their death or disability, but it is important to handle early. You need a plan now, no matter what age you are or your current health. Your plan will protect both you and your loved ones, so put the time in now, even if it is hard.

15

NO-BABY STEP 7

PLAN FOR MOM AND DAD

Do you plan on caring for family members in the future?

"My sister and I have an agreement. I will pay for most of the expenses; she will provide most of the care. We are currently under contract on a house for our parents. This will give them a place to live for now and will help to cover costs of long-term care in the future."

—SELENA, FORTY, SINGLE

It may seem odd that your financial plan should include planning for your parents, but their financial and medical needs may have more of an impact on your financial plan than your own choices. While you may have heard about the sandwich generation (people taking care of their kids and parents at the same time), Childfree folks are the open-faced sandwich (caring for our parents). We need to watch out for the financial BINGO ("You don't have kids, so you can take care of Mom."), and have a plan for life, finances, and care for our parents.

BOUNDARIES

In the first section of the book on life planning, I touched on setting good boundaries with your parents and the ways you will (or won't) care for them. Setting boundaries is so important that I want to bring it up again and dive in a bit deeper. Our parents and family know the buttons to push and are great at booking us on guilt trips. Even if they aren't intentionally booking guilt trips for you, society, culture, and others may inadvertently push you. Each time someone tries to guilt you into doing something you don't want to do, you need to push back on your boundaries and hold fast.

Emergencies and acute events make it hard to keep our boundaries. Mom may have fallen, broken her hip, and needed a couple weeks of help. You move in with her, or she moves in with you, and you both work on her recovery. Historically, when you stop moving, such as with a hip fracture, other things start going wrong. Eventually, you look back and it has been months instead of weeks that you have been caring for her, and you lost yourself somewhere in the middle. If you don't break the cycle, all of your boundaries will be gone, and you will be caring for Mom for the rest of her life.

If you are okay caring for parents for life, more power to you. But you will need to set caring for them as a goal in your financial plan and set aside some of your other goals. The key is for it to be a deliberate decision. You get to pick your own goals and boundaries; just be strong in whatever you pick.

A word of caution for couples: I've been taking care of my mother in one way or another all my life. My sister and I have a system in place to provide support, work with hospitals and doctors, and somehow try to maintain the balance with our own lives. Even though I live 1,200 miles away from my mother now, my sister and I talk enough to know when I need to visit to keep an eye on things or not. I sometimes forget that my wife did not grow up with the same experiences. It is normal for me to drop everything and head to the hospital. It is not a freak-out moment for me, as I'm used to it. I'm used to hanging in emergency rooms and come prepared with my phone and a charger. My wife faints at the sight of blood and sometimes gets queasy when visiting the hospital. While as a couple we have good boundaries about how we will and won't help, it is key to remember that we all have different comfort levels and skills when it comes to caregiving, and it is important to communicate and understand how each of you feels about it.

GETTING YOUR PARENTS' PAPERWORK SET UP

No matter what boundary you set, you need to make sure your parents' paperwork is in place. You need a copy of their wills, POAs, and in-case-I-die files. If they have medical issues, you may also want a copy of their medical records and a Vial of Life, which is a basic set of medical conditions, medicines, and other information for emergency medical services (often kept in the fridge, so there is a common place to find it, but you should also have a copy with you). The hard part may not be getting a copy of the paperwork but getting your parents to complete their paperwork in the first place.

Many people struggle with starting the conversation with their parents. It is an odd conversation to be sure and has a lot of baggage in it. The hardest part is often just starting the conversation, so let me give you a free tool—blame me. That's right—you can say, "I've been reading about financial planning and Dr. Jay says I need to talk to you about your estate plan and finances." They will probably laugh and ask who the heck Dr. Jay is, but it gets the conversation started.

You will probably also have to tell them that you are asking about their will and other paperwork because you are trying to take care of them, not because you are worrying about your inheritance.

Unfortunately, there is still some taboo around discussing finances, and that can be amplified when you are talking to family and friends. If your parents adamantly refuse to discuss things with you, make sure you connect them with an advice-only or flat-fee CFP® professional and an estate or elder lawyer.

If your parents do not have any paperwork in place, their process will look much like yours in No-Baby Step 6. You can help walk them through the discussions and even help with filling out the forms online. Just remember that if you are in the will, or will be acting as executor or POA, you will need someone else to witness the will signing.

If they have paperwork in place (or need some help), here are some questions to ask. The list below is not exhaustive but should get you talking about what matters.

Is there a will (and can I have a copy)? Who is the executor of the will and the backup? Are there any specific wishes we need to follow? (Ask about family heirlooms, or anything that has special meaning. Also, ask about burial wishes.)

Is there a healthcare directive (and can I have a copy)? Who is your medical POA and backup? (NOTE: With POAs you want a primary and backup, not an either/or situation. For example, if Mom lists both of her kids as POA with an "or," then it can result in split decisions and fights.) When and how do you want us to step in to help?

Do you have a financial POA (and can I have a copy)? Who is the POA and backup? When and how do you want us to step in to help?

What is your plan for long-term care? Do you have long-term care insurance? (NOTE: If they have long-term care [LTC] insurance, you may want to take over managing the payments to make sure they are always paid. You don't want them to miss a payment and lose coverage.)

Do you have life insurance or other insurance policies? Who are the beneficiaries? (NOTE: Make sure to check that their beneficiaries are updated and match their wishes.)

Where are all your financial and bank accounts? Can I be listed on them as a trusted contact (more on that later)? Do you have any safe deposit boxes? (NOTE: It is really important to find out about safe deposit boxes, as they can be hard to find and access without information and paperwork. The nightmare situation is if they keep their will in the safe deposit box, which you can only access if you know it exists and have permission to get into it.)

What are your retirement accounts, and do you have any pensions? Who are the beneficiaries on your accounts? (Be sure to verify these.)

Do you have gold, silver, cash, or other valuables anywhere? (NOTE: My neighbor is still looking for $250K+ in gold his father buried somewhere without telling his kids where it was before he passed. Take this as a cautionary tale.)

Do you have any paper stock certificates? How about crypto wallets?

What bills and debt do you have? Are they on automatic payment? If not, can we set that up for you?

Is there anything else you would like to share? (NOTE: This is a great opportunity to have those heart-to-heart talks you need to have or to clear the air about anything.)

I can't think of every question you should ask your parents, but the ones here give you a place to start. It also will likely be an ongoing discussion. Sometimes it is easier to have these discussions facilitated by a third person. The only parents I take now as clients are parents of my Childfree people. I do that to help both my clients (the Childfree people) and their parents. It is very common to "find" things over time that your parents may not have mentioned. I tend to ask the same questions four or five different ways, and I often get different answers. For example, I recently had an elderly client ask me about buying gold (after they saw it on TV). After talking about gold, I asked a few questions and found they had probably $30K in silver coins in buckets in their closet that no one knew about. Keep asking questions.

All this paperwork and questioning is easier to do before your parents are showing any type of cognitive decline. That is why it is important to start now. If they have started to decline, you will need to contact an elder-care lawyer to help you with their paperwork. You will also have to watch their mail closely (and email if you have access) to make sure you are not missing anything. You may also want to sign up for USPS Informed Delivery so that you get a scan of all incoming mail and can watch out for important items.

NAVIGATING SIBLINGS AND FAMILY DISPUTES

If you have siblings or other close family, you need to be sure they are well informed about who is making decisions for your parents. It does not have to be you, but someone needs to make the decisions. They also need to know what your parents' wishes are and how they can help. In some families, one sibling might do the physical care of their parents while the other provides financial support. In other families, one person does everything, and the rest of the family does not show up until inheritance checks are available (which is very sad).

I've seen way too many families destroyed by money and inheritances. I've heard of people asking for their check from the will before their loved one is even buried. I've seen people fight over minuscule amounts, and family feuds start over small things. The only way to try to prevent this is to have a discussion up front and make sure the paperwork matches.

UNDERSTANDING MEDICARE AND MEDICAID

The key thing to remember is that Medicare does not cover long-term care and Medicaid kicks in only after you have spent all your money. If your parents are going to end up on Medicaid, you may want to consult an elder law attorney from the state they live in. An elder law attorney can help you to identify if there is anything you can do to protect their assets from Medicaid. The challenge with Medicaid is that there is a five-year look back in most cases, meaning Medicaid will look at any financial transactions or gifts that occurred in the past five years to determine if you are eligible, so you need to act well in advance of your parents needing Medicaid care. For example, if your parents gave you all of their money three years ago, Medicaid could say they are not eligible until that money is spent or five years have passed from when they moved it.

I've seen way too many people try to "hide" things from Medicaid to protect assets and their inheritance. There are a lot of old wives' tales about how to protect yourself from Medicaid. The most common is to just put the house in the kids' names to protect it. This may work as long as it is done more than five years before they go on Medicaid, but it has issues. The core issue is that Medicaid care sucks.

As a paramedic, I always knew when we were in a Medicaid facility because the floors are sticky and there are four people in each room. Not all facilities are this way, but Medicaid pays less than those who are paying by cash or long-term care insurance, and you can see the difference. So, the question becomes, is your focus on protecting your inheritance or caring for your elderly parents? You may be able to protect their house from being taken, but maybe they would be better off selling the house and paying for good care out of pocket.

On the flip side, if your parents have no assets, lots of debt, and/or very little income, Medicaid is their only choice. At that point, your goal should be to get them in the best available Medicaid facility or possibly care for them in your home or theirs.

YOUR PARENTS' FINANCIAL SITUATION

With the hard questions answered, you will have an idea of your parents' overall financial situation. It is not a scientific measure, but you will probably have a gut reaction that falls into one of three buckets:

They are doing well. Your parents have enough money and a plan to cover long-term care and will probably have enough to leave you an inheritance.

They are okay but will end up on Medicaid. Your parents have enough money to make it through, but their long-term care will be paid by Medicaid.

They are in rough shape. Your parents are struggling, and you will probably need to help them and get support from state and federal programs (including Medicaid).

Unfortunately, there are so many factors that go into your parents' finances that I can't create a simple chart that puts them into these three buckets, but your guess is probably close. You may be able to help nudge your parents up one level, but often their financial plan is relatively set.

Helping them with their finances

At some point, your parents may need help with their finances. This may just be in helping them to coordinate paying their bills or may require you to chip in with your own money. Be sure to keep strong to your boundaries. There is normally a progression from you keeping an eye on things, to helping them day in day out, and then finally to handling things completely. Many times, it is easier to just take over everything, but that may not fit you or your parents' wishes.

The first step is to get listed as a "trusted person" on their accounts. A trusted person is someone the bank (or other financial institution) can call if something odd is going on in their account. A trusted person doesn't have control over their finances (as opposed to a POA, who does), but it is a bit of a speed bump if anything is going wrong. Here's an example: A woman in her eighties started dating someone half her age, and she began taking out $20K regularly from her bank account. The bank contacted the trusted person (her daughter). The daughter talked to her mom, and while the daughter did not agree with it, her mom kept taking out large amounts of money. The bottom line is that the daughter could not stop her, but she was at least aware of what was going on and could talk to her mom about it.

Another option I hear frequently is to just add your name to your parents' accounts. Adding your name may be problematic. Just having your name on the account does not give you the notifications that a trusted person might get. Also, there are tax implications. When you get added, you may be seen to have gotten a gift from the account and will be responsible for paying taxes on interest and other income from the account. The last issue is that anyone on a joint account can drain it, so there is a potential for abuse and other issues.

The best answer is to get listed as a trusted person and to have a financial POA. With a financial POA, you are effectively signing on behalf of them. You can get access to the account (in person and online) and keep an eye on things. You can also handle any bill paying in this way.

When you start paying bills for your parents (with your money or theirs), it is best to take over all their finances. You don't want two people writing checks from the same account, as that is how you end up either missing a bill or double paying.

Contributing to their finances

My wife and I have a hard-and-fast rule that we don't give money to anyone. We will buy loved ones groceries, help pay their medical bills, and help them in other ways, but no cash. The reason is simple: we can't control what they spend cash on. You don't have to agree with our rules, and that's fine; you can set your own. The bottom line is that it is your money, and you get to decide what you want to do with it. There are a couple of things you need to keep in mind if you are going to help financially.

First, you need to be mindful of gift taxes. In 2024, you could give $18,000 to someone without paying taxes. Above that amount you as the giver either need to pay taxes or use part of your estate gift tax exclusion (you file that with your taxes). If you are in a couple and do gift splitting, you can each give $18,000, and if you are giving to both sets of your parents, you can effectively give them $72,000 per year (4 x $18,000). That sounds like a lot, but depending on what they need, it may not cover everything. The one good thing is that you can pay medical bills directly and get around gift taxes. Depending on the situation, you may be able to count them as dependents also. (Consult your tax professional for more information.)

Second, you need to be mindful of your own finances. Even if you are not giving directly, caring for parents can be costly. You may need to take time off work to care for them or take them to appointments. You may cover housing expenses if they move in with you. You may just pick up a bill here and there, but it adds up. The key is to track both your direct and indirect expenses and keep them within your budget (and boundaries).

COHABITATING WITH YOUR PARENTS

My wife and I also have a hard-and-fast rule that no one moves in with us. I have enough trouble sharing our space with our pets; forget sharing it with another family member. We don't really have a hard rule about moving in with parents, but I don't see that happening either. We will help pay for care if they need it though.

Living with your parents is a HUGE decision. My only real advice would be to avoid it, if possible, but that is often not realistic. It is relatively common to see soloists move in with their parents to care for them. The problem is that what seems like a short-term solution can quickly become decades of a life they did not have planned.

It is also becoming common for people to build (or buy) an in-law or accessory apartment on their property for their aging parents. Many states have even set up expedited approval processes for these add-ons. It is probably the best choice if you have the money and space. With an accessory apartment your parents are close enough for you to give support yet far enough that you have some privacy and can keep some semblance of the life you wanted to live.

The third option that is growing in popularity is "care villages." They have become very popular in sunny states with lots of retirees. In these facilities, there is a continuum of care from independent living through to skilled care. If you believe your parents need a bit of help, but not full care yet, start with looking at a village. They tend to have group events, meals, and more, which many people enjoy. You can offer to help pay for your parents to move in there and know they are in good hands.

CAREGIVING AND CAREGIVER FATIGUE

I can't talk about caring for your parents without talking about caregiver fatigue. We can each only handle so much. You need to remember that you are your own person first before you are a caregiver. And as a caregiver, you should be your parents' child first, then a caregiver. Your role is to help and support your parents, not to do everything for them. You need to know your own limits and be okay saying when you have had enough.

Knowing your role and limits can be particularly hard if you have a healthcare background. You want to be an advocate for your parents and their health, but you don't want to be one of their medical caregivers. The problem is if you are a registered nurse (RN) (or other medical professional), there may be an assumption, both by family and health-care providers, that you can take care of everything. For example, they may expect you to do wound dressing if you have medical skills, where in other cases they would have a home care nurse come in to take care of it. You need to set and keep boundaries.

Plan for breaks. If you are your parents' 24/7 caregiver, you need to have scheduled time off. It might be as easy as asking another family member to cover dinners and one day out of the weekend so that you can get a break. In other cases, it may require you to pay for help, but you need to find time for yourself.

GET HELP BY CREATING A TEAM

In the end, caregiving requires a team. Other family members can be part of that team. Everyone can have different roles and responsibilities, but we are all part of the team. You will want to leverage any and all available resources. This can include state and federal assistance in addition to fees for other caregivers and support. Here are some supports to think about:

Local, county, or state social worker: Your local city or county may have a social worker who can help you with understanding what your parents may qualify for. There are a wide variety of assistance programs available, so make sure you get some help on how to apply successfully.

Hospital or insurance social worker: If your parent has considerable health issues, they may be assigned a social worker by the hospital or their insurance. I've seen mixed results with these social workers, as they ultimately represent the person who pays them (and not you). Use what you can, but question things.

Aging care manager: Aging care managers come with a variety of skills, but you can think about them as a social worker you hire to represent you and your parent. They can help fight with the insurance companies and make care suggestions. It may take you a while to find the right one for you, as good aging care managers are busy, but you can start at the Aging Life Care Association website.

Veterans Administration: If your parent served in the military or ever qualified for VA benefits, be sure to reach out and see what they qualify for. There are Veteran Service Officers in each state who can help with the process.

CERTIFIED FINANCIAL PLANNER™: It can be tough to balance your parents' finances and yours. You may want to hire a CFP® to help you to set a plan for them, particularly around paying taxes, spending down their retirement, and paying for long-term care.

Certified public accountant (CPA)/tax preparer: You will also want a paid tax preparer to help you with your parents' taxes. Taxes and tax planning become a big issue, especially when it comes to figuring out required minimum distributions and estate tax plans.

If it sounds like there is a lot to think about in No-Baby Step 7, it is because there is. Whatever plan you set for Mom and Dad will likely change, but the more you can plan in advance, the better off you are.

DIVING DEEPER: For more, visit https://childfreewealth.com/134.

16

NO-BABY STEP 8

WIND DOWN YOUR WEALTH

What is the best thing about being Childfree?

"The ability to make on-the-whim decisions in your day-to-day life or financially. You can take risks without having to worry about someone else's life and well-being. Having the time, finances, and bandwidth to take care of yourself and your mental health."

—HANNAH, TWENTY-FIVE, LONG-TERM RELATIONSHIP

Now that you have reached No-Baby Step 8, it is time to shift your entire approach to life and finances, and that is not an exaggeration. In the financial literature, they would say you have moved from the accumulation phase to the deaccumulation phase. That is fancy wording for saying that you need to start spending more than you save or earn. The problem is, the skills and behaviors you used to get you here are different from the ones you will use for the rest of your life.

DIVING DEEPER: For more, visit https://childfreewealth.com/135.

ONCE YOU'VE HIT YOUR GOALS

When you get to No-Baby Step 8 (or slightly before), you may experience the Childfree Midlife crisis, where you've hit your personal, professional, and financial goals. I mentioned this in the life planning section, but here is where you actually need to do something about it. Here is where you hit all the hard questions about the meaning of life, what you want to do when you grow up, what your goals are, what you want your life to be, what your impact will be, and more.

Go back to your life plan and look at what you said mattered before you started the No-Baby Steps. Chances are some of it will still fit, while some no longer will, and that is okay. You aren't stuck with decisions you made in the past. It is time to start looking forward and enjoying life. Oh yeah, and you need to spend and give away some money.

NET WORTH

The key when you get to this step is to watch your net worth and portfolio return. Net worth is simply everything you own minus everything you owe. If you are debt free, it is just everything you own. If you own a house, that gets included as an asset (although a mortgage is considered debt). Going forward, you are going to use your net worth to track your progress. There are four milestones for net worth that I watch closely for my clients:

Negative net worth: If you have debt, you can have a negative net worth (owe more than you own). Getting from a negative net worth to zero is often the hardest step.

Zero net worth: Getting to zero is a major milestone. Many Americans may never make it this far.

$100K net worth: Having a $100K net worth means you are actively saving and investing for your future. Your money is starting to work for you.

$1 million net worth: You are a millionaire. At this point, your net worth is growing on its own, and you get to start making decisions about where you want to go with it.

If you have a zero or negative net worth, getting to $1 million may seem like a dream. It is not. It is just a reflection of doing the right things over time and letting your money grow. Once you hit your first million, all too often it will seem like no big deal. I love adding up someone's net worth and declaring them a millionaire, as it usually hasn't "sunk in" yet to them, and it doesn't feel much different.

As you get over $1 million net worth, and possibly before, you may hit the "tipping point." The tipping point is when your investments are making more for you than your salary. The exact point is different for everyone, but it is somewhat humbling when you realize you can make more money doing nothing than at your job. It is usually at this point that every extra dollar you earn starts to go to your estate, which is not a priority for most Childfree people. It is a sign that something needs to change.

The caution here is that once you hit $1 million, or whatever your goal was, people tend to move the goalposts. It becomes something like, "Well, I made it to a million, and that isn't much, so let's shoot for two million." Once they hit $2 million, the goal becomes $5 million, then $10 million, then...STOP! Seriously! Adding more money isn't going to make you happier, and it is just going to cause you estate tax problems.

If you are embracing the concepts of winding down your debt, you need to set your safety net (outlined in the next section) and then start bending the net worth curve down, not up. The problem is that if you have achieved your net worth goals, you have built good skills in saving money and now you need to learn how to give and spend.

This is when working with a CFP® with good financial planning software can help you. I've seen this cycle so many times that I can predict how it goes.

I meet with my clients monthly, and we work on one to two things. Often, they will reach out because they are concerned about something, like running out of money. I will build out their financial plan in our software, confirm they want to die with zero, set their safety net, and then tell them they are okay. It is at that point that they freak out. They ask me dozens of questions and what-ifs. I'll run through all of them and show them they are okay. After about three or so meetings, they will finally buy into the plan, numbers, and simulations, and then their head explodes. We then spend our time talking about giving, spending, and enjoying their life. I've had people in their thirties reach this point and others in their sixties. It is always the same in that it leaves them bewildered about what to do next, as most of the financial literature focuses on saving, not spending. That is when the fun starts.

You will most likely hit this point also. If you build out your plan in financial planning software, it will often give you the option to do a Monte Carlo simulation. In a Monte Carlo simulation, it runs a thousand (or so) simulations from the market being better than ever or worse than ever. It will then give you a score. For example, it might say you have a 95% chance of success. The problem for us is that you need to invert that, as Monte Carlo considers it a success if you DON'T run out of money. If you want to die with zero, then a 95% success on a Monte Carlo is actually a 95% chance of failure.

With all your numbers in some good planning software, you can play with how much you would have to spend to run out of money. If you plan on keeping an eye on your finances (and making changes as needed), then you can shoot for a 50% success in the Monte Carlo simulations. Or you can set up a guardrail system. In a guardrail system, you determine the minimum you need to spend each year, plus or minus how the market did last year. At its simplest, you need to spend more than your investments bring in to bend the curve.

Side note: Keep in mind that most (nearly all) financial software assumes you don't want to run out of money, so you will have to make some serious adjustments and judgments (which is why a CFP® can help). Even a common rule like the 4% safe withdrawal rule assumes you want to keep your nest egg, so watch the general rules.

DIVING DEEPER: For more, visit https://childfreewealth.com/100.

SAFETY NET

Okay, I know you don't really want to die with exactly zero dollars. The point isn't about having nothing in your accounts at the end, and you certainly don't want to run out of money before you die. So that is why we build a safety net by:

Having a plan for long-term care
Putting off collecting Social Security until seventy years old
Putting aside a cash cushion

You should have built a plan for long-term care in No-Baby Step 6, so the first part should be done. The point is to have a long-term care plan established well in advance, so it doesn't sneak up on you and suck all of your money dry at the end of life. If you are on the opt-out plan, this will also change the need for a cash cushion.

The second part of your safety net is putting off collecting Social Security until seventy years old. The reason we put off collecting is that you will get the biggest monthly payment at seventy, and Social Security has a built-in inflation system. Social Security has some problems (discussed later, along with other options), but if it is going to be there, you may want to use it as part of your safety net. For myself, I plan on putting it off until seventy, but I discount the amount I will receive by 25% to reflect current issues in the system.

The last part of your safety net is a cash cushion. The point of this cushion is to make you feel comfortable that you will have money if you need it, especially if you think there will be issues with Social Security. I don't have an exact number to recommend, as it varies based upon your expenses and assumptions. You can start by doing a cushion of one to three years of expenses. Set that amount aside and invest it like everything else. Keep in mind that the type of account (taxable, tax-advantaged) will have an impact, and if you use a traditional account, you may run into a required minimum distribution (RMD) issue. If you happen to have a Roth account with somewhere near the right amount, that would be perfect, as in general you should use your Roth funds last.

WHAT TO DO WITH THE REST

With your safety net in place, it is time to start giving and spending it. You get to choose what amounts you give and spend. I believe giving to the people and causes you believe in can be just as rewarding as, if not more than, spending the money yourself. Therefore, a good place to start is to give away the same amount as you spend. You can adjust the percentages as you go along. You might not be exactly equal each year, and it may make sense to bunch your giving into certain years (for tax purposes), but over the rest of your life, it should work itself out.

Giving

Giving is going to fall into one of two buckets: to charities—501(c)(3)s and the like—and everyone else. The reason I split giving into two buckets is that you want to get as much tax benefit as you can for your giving. I want you to create your giving plan without focusing on the taxes, but once you decide, you should try to get whatever tax benefits you can. Here are some questions that may help you think about giving options:

Who (or what organization) helped me in my life? Can I return the favor or sponsor others in the same situation?

Who in my family, friends, or society as a whole would I like to help? How can I best help them?

What causes am I passionate about? Can I best help them with my money, time, or some other way?

Is there anyone in my family, like parents or others, who I would like to have an impact on? (NOTE: If you get an inheritance, this question is great as you are thinking through what they would want done with the money.)

How can I help people indirectly with my money?

Do I want credit for my giving?

There are a lot more questions you can ask yourself, but those should get you started on a list. Let me give you a couple examples from my giving plan:

For family members, I don't give money directly, but I will provide indirect support. It is amazing how much you can help someone by placing an Instacart order for them (and paying for it of course). I also tend to give a lot of time to helping family and friends.

We have a 529 College Savings Plan for our nephews. We started donating to the fund each month for our nephews in the hopes that it will help when they go to college (or some other school).

I truly enjoy random acts of kindness. The classic example of this is leaving a giant tip for someone who is struggling, but it can be so much more. My heart goes out to those people who work hard, struggle, and never ask for anything. I will go out of my way to find a way to help them with my time, training, or money.

My community efforts now are wrapped around supporting Childfree people. Both in my business and personal life, I'm working to give the Childfree community a voice and resources. I also regularly hold pro bono financial planning sessions for Childfree people who need it.

My favorite nonprofit organization right now is Undue Medical Debt. My parents always struggled with medical debt, so it fits

> my heart. You can donate to them, and they buy medical debt for pennies on the dollar and then forgive it. It means you can get a one hundred times impact on your donations.

Your giving plan won't look like mine, and that is okay. The point is to figure out who you want to help and how. Once you have your plan in place, the next step is to figure out the best way to get a tax break from your giving. In my example, at times we have been able to get a tax break for the 529 deduction (depends by state), we can deduct donations to the nonprofit, and some of the work in the Childfree community can be a business marketing deduction. We don't get tax breaks for the rest, and that is perfectly fine.

DIVING DEEPER: For more, visit https://childfreewealth.com/90.

GIVING TO PEOPLE

When it comes to giving to people, you are not likely to get any tax benefits. There are always exceptions (like the 529 plan, or if you claim them as a dependent) but those are rare. The bigger issue with giving to people is in staying out of gift and estate taxes. Just as with your parents, in 2024, you can give $18,000 to anyone, tax free, and if you and your spouse gift split that goes up to $36,000. Gift splitting is as simple as checking a box on your tax return, but it means that you can each give $18K to one person for a total of $36K. If you absolutely must give more in one year, be sure to talk to your CPA or tax preparer to use up your gift and estate tax exemption. You can also pay medical and tuition expenses directly and get around the gift tax issues.

People sometimes get weird when it comes to giving and receiving gifts, especially money. Instead, you may want to think about how you can help them indirectly. They may not be willing to accept $5,000 for a vacation but may be willing to join you in the oversized house you rented on the beach for a vacation.

You can also buy them services and support. I've seen people pay for house cleaning, replacement appliances, house painting, and more. I've also had people pay for life and career coaches, CFP® professionals, CPAs, and other professionals to help their family when they are struggling. It doesn't have to be fancy or expensive. I had someone who was worried that their sibling can't drive anymore. They set up an Uber account for their sibling (billed to themselves, of course) and allowed their sibling to use it as they saw fit. The result was that the issue was resolved, at a reasonable cost, and everyone felt better.

You may also be better off giving your time than your money to others. I have a particular skill in finance, and I've done a lot of work with people who are disabled. People who are disabled have both medical and financial concerns but may not be able to pay for professional help. Those are the people I go out of my way to help. What skills do you have that could help others? Is there someone you could coach or mentor? Is there a group of people you would like to help?

Keep in mind that you can help people a lot more while you are alive than after you pass. If there is someone you would like to leave money to after you pass, then give it to them now, when they can use it better. As long as you maintain your safety net, you will be okay. For example, if I live until my eighties, my nephews will be in their fifties when I die.

Chances are they may not need the money then, and they could have really used it earlier in their life to get them set up for success.

Find the right way to help your loved one and do it now. Think of it this way: I'm a big fan of education, but it is not affordable for everyone. Maybe you can pay for someone to go back to school, get a degree or certification, or even just work with a coach and achieve more with their life (by their measure, not yours). That will have a much larger impact on their entire life than getting $100K when you die.

GIVING TO CHARITIES

Giving to charities can be a good way to not only help people but to also get a tax break. Once you know what charities you want to donate to, you can check the IRS website to see if it qualifies for a deduction. For 501(c)(3) organizations, it is also a good idea to check their form 990, which is filed publicly and outlines their finances. You may be surprised by how some organizations use their money (and it usually isn't a good surprise).

From a tax perspective, it is usually best to "bunch" donations. What that means is you make a big donation one year and then take a year or two off from donations. The result is that you may be able to take advantage of the standard deduction in "off" years and the charitable deduction in other years.

Fortunately, there is a way to make a charitable donation in one year and give away the money you donated over future years. You can set up a donor-advised fund (DAF) at Vanguard and many other places. With a DAF, you get credit for the donation this year; then you can invest the money and give it away as you find the right charities. There are limitations on who you can donate to, but most of the IRS list should work.

The other bonus with a DAF is that you may be able to donate appreciated stock. This means that if you follow the advice here—buy stock and held on to it forever—you can donate that stock to a DAF (or other charity) without paying capital gains tax. It allows your money to go farther and saves you on taxes.

Another giving option is to do qualified charitable distributions (QCDs). With a QCD, once you hit seventy and a half years old, you can donate up to $105,000 (in 2024) to a charity directly from your traditional IRA, and it can be in place of your required minimum distributions (RMDs). The bottom line is that you may be able to donate instead of paying taxes on your RMDs.

What if the charity is not on the IRS list? You can still make a donation; it just may not be tax deductible. For example, I've regularly had people who want to donate to a cause outside the United States. Unless they have a 501(c)(3) or similar in the United States that you can donate to, that donation is not going to have a tax benefit. You can, and probably should, still make the donation if it is for the person you want to help.

I'm sure by now you may be overwhelmed by all the IRS speak in relation to charitable giving. The truth is, I haven't even touched the tip of the iceberg. There are so many ways to do charitable giving that it is a good place to work with an advice-only or flat-fee CFP® professional and your tax preparer for professional advice.

DIVING DEEPER: For more, visit https://childfreewealth.com/91.

Spending

Someone is going to read this and think, *Really? You included a section on spending your money? That's the easy part...* The reality is that if you have been a saver for life, spending is a skill you have to learn (or relearn). I mentioned the blueberry problem earlier, and here is where it comes out. You can start with small spending increases and work your way up to what you really want.

Here's a great example: If you travel, start flying business or first class. Once you do, you won't go back to economy. It will feel like a splurge, and it kind of is, but you will enjoy your trips that much more.

Here's another: Start spending money to get your time back. Think about getting a housekeeper, landscaper, dog walker, or someone to do whatever you don't want to do. I've even had people pay for a personal chef to make all their meals. It tends to be cheaper than eating out, and you get to have them make your favorites at home, with your preferences in mind.

The point is not to spend mindlessly but to set a goal to spend money on the things you enjoy. If you enjoy travel, maybe you budget $50K to 100K per year on travel. That may sound like a lot to some, but to others that will barely move the needle. Set the rate at your budget and within your guardrails. You can then either travel more often or travel better; I chose to travel better.

I mentioned earlier that I want to buy a Nordhavn 51 boat and travel the world. Buying a boat is a terrible financial decision, but you can definitely spend money there. If we end up having more money when it is time to travel the world, who knows, I might buy a bigger boat or pay for a crew to help us. The options are endless. Not everyone has a big spending goal, and not everyone wants to buy one big item like I do. That is okay. Pick what matters to you. My wife would probably spend it all on pets, and we'd have a whole rescue sanctuary in our house.

QUITTING YOUR JOB AND EMBRACING THE FINANCIAL INDEPENDENCE, LIVE EARLY (FILE) LIFESTYLE

The other option for No-Baby Step 8 is to truly embrace the Financial Independence, Live Early (FILE) lifestyle and make a big change. Invest in yourself. Change jobs, start a business, go back to school, start that nonprofit, volunteer, whatever! You can get paid for the new job, or not—who cares. You could write that great novel and see where it goes. You can move to another country and work remotely. The options are endless.

The fact that the options are endless can itself be a problem. FILE is about thinking differently about work and life and achieving a balance. Many of us (myself included) are not good at work-life balance. I mean right now, I'm sitting on my boat, writing this book, when I really should just be out on the lake enjoying myself. I hope one day to find the balance in my own life, and I hope you find it in yours.

Remember that with the die-with-zero safety net in place, you can take chances. It is okay if you try something and fail. Just be sure to get back up and try something else. Got a wild idea? Go try it!

IMPACT

The final question is always this: What impact do you want to make on yourself, your family, your friends, and the world? I'm not going to get all sappy here, but this is often the question that we struggle with in our later years. What you want to leave an impact on may change over time, especially if you succeed at something.

Leaving money in your estate is one way to make an impact, but how much more of an impact can you make with a giving and spending plan? What memories can you make for yourself? What lives can you improve? What experiences can you have (either by yourself or with others)? What do you want your tombstone to say?

These are the questions you can ask yourself along the way to help guide your decisions in your later years. And remember that it's fluid: the kind of impact you want to make when you're twenty could be vastly different from what you feel strongly or care about in your seventies. And that's okay. One idea is to keep a journal, where you can sift through your thinking over time and ultimately arrive at the impact you want to make.

The No-Baby Steps will take you through the core of financial planning, but they will not cover everything. In the following sections, I dive deeper into specific topics that may or may not apply to you. Tax planning, for example, applies to most everyone but will depend on your own personal situation. There is no need to read all the sections beyond here if they do not apply to you. Just pick the ones that fit you, and know you have resources for when your life and financial plans change. Consider these sections "extra credit" if you want.

PART III

TAXES AND OTHER CONSIDERATIONS

17
TAX PLANNING

What is the best thing about being Childfree?

"Not having to spend money on something that doesn't directly benefit myself, my partner, or our pets."

—MARIA, TWENTY-FOUR, COUPLE NOT MARRIED

Investing can be very simple. You can follow the three-fund portfolio plan, maybe invest in a target date fund in your 401(k), set and forget it. While you can make your investing more complex, and can always learn more, more complexity is not likely to make a difference.

Taxes and tax planning, on the other hand, are complex by nature and can have a huge impact on your financial plan over your lifetime. Tax planning is an area where you will want some professional help. I'm going to try to give you some basics, things to watch out for, and some things to think about so that you know when to call for help. My intent is not to make you a tax expert but to help you understand the thought process. Keep in mind that the tax law changes every year, so take everything here as basic concepts, not hard-and-fast numbers or rules.

If you are reading this section hoping that I will have some tax scheme to get you out of paying taxes completely, you will be disappointed. My take on taxes is to follow the rules exactly, earn every deduction you can, and pay them on time. That may sound boring, but it is the only way. You don't want someone to be "creative" with your taxes. Remember, your signature is at the bottom, so if that creative idea does not work out, you are on the hook. At the same time, let's not give the IRS a tip—they get exactly what they are owed, and not a penny more.

TAX PLANNING VS. TAX FILING

There is a huge difference between filing your taxes each year and doing tax planning. There are decisions you can make that will save you taxes on this year's return but will cost you more in the long run. We don't get a choice of whether we need to pay taxes or not, but we do sometimes get a choice about when and in what form. Picking the right taxes to pay and when to pay them is at the core of tax planning.

You may find that your tax filer—a certified public accountant (CPA) or an enrolled agent (EA)—may conflict with your CERTIFIED FINANCIAL PLANNER™ and their tax plan. The problem is that the CPA or EA may file taxes but may not do tax planning, while the financial planner does tax planning but usually does not do tax filing. Tax filing and tax planning are two different skills. Besides having different skill sets, the other cause of disagreement is that much of the tax code is up to interpretation, and what makes sense from a tax purpose and from a financial perspective may be different. As a CERTIFIED FINANCIAL PLANNER™, I will defer to someone's CPA when it comes to filing taxes and in interpreting tax rules. On the flip side, CPAs will often defer to us on investments.

What does that mean for you? It means you need to have a team of professionals to help you as your finances get more complex. When you just have your W-2 (regular income) employment and a small number of investments, you can probably do your taxes on your own. As your income and net worth grow, and your tax return becomes more complex, it is time to get help. If you run a small business or other side gig, get a professional to help.

DIVING DEEPER: For more, visit https://childfreewealth.com/49.

TAX BASICS

The Tax Cut and Jobs Act (TCJA) came into effect January 1, 2018, and simplified taxes for many. When the TCJA was put into effect, it doubled the standard deduction to $14,600 for single filers and $29,200 for married couples filing jointly (2024 numbers). At the same time, it imposed a cap on state and local taxes of $10,000. The result was that an estimated 90% of filers now take the standard deduction. You probably took the standard deduction last year (or could have).

What that means to you is that the game of itemizing deductions doesn't work for many people now. The problem is that many people still think about itemizing their taxes even though they don't. For example, you can deduct mortgage interest, but if you take the standard deduction, you get nothing extra off for having a mortgage. Even though this has been the case since 2018, you will still hear people talking about deducting their mortgage interest.

The fact that most people use the standard deduction is also why I recommend bunching up your charitable donations into one big deduction. The result is that you take the standard deduction most years and itemize deductions when you are making a large charitable contribution.

You can still get some tax credits above and beyond the standard deduction, but they are few and far between for Childfree people. Every year at tax time, I hear Childfree people complaining about not being able to claim the child tax credit. Here's what you need to keep in mind: The child tax credit in 2024 was $3,995 per child. At the same time, the national average cost of having a kid was $25,000 per year or more.[8] You don't have to be a math or finance genius to see that the credit does not make up for the cost.

Another thing to keep in mind about the child tax credit is that the U.S. government uses the tax code to encourage behaviors (by giving tax breaks) and discourage others. Our current tax code definitely has a pronatalist bias. It has a bias because our economy, tax system, and Social Security are all based upon constant population growth. In the Social Security chapter, I will dive deeper into this, but without constant growth, the entire system may be at risk. I'm not going to get too political, but in my mind, the answer is to fix the system, not rely on enough babies constantly being born, but just remember that it is built into your taxes and Social Security.

---

8 Tim Parker, "How Much Does It Cost to Raise a Child in the U.S.?" Investopedia, accessed November 16, 2023, https://www.investopedia.com/articles/personal-finance/090415/cost-raising-child-america.asp.

Remember, getting a bigger refund should not be your goal. If you are getting a big refund, that means that you overpaid and gave the U.S. government a tax-free loan. For my clients, I usually try to get within $500 of their tax bill (either owe or get a refund of $500). If you regularly either get a lot back or owe a lot, you need to adjust your withholding or estimated tax payments.

While the United States has a very complex tax system, your own personal taxes will be made up of a combination of income taxes and capital gains taxes. In most cases, income taxes are going to be higher than long-term capital gains, so if you have a choice, try to pay long-term capital gains.

DIVING DEEPER: For more, visit https://childfreewealth.com/41.

Income tax

The United States is one of very few countries that tax you on your worldwide income. What that means is that if you are a U.S. citizen, you pay income taxes on everything you earn, no matter where in the world you earn it, unless it is specifically exempt by law. The IRS does not care how you earned your money and will even tax you on money that you stole or gained by other illegal means. Giving up your citizenship will not save you, as you will then have to pay an "exit tax" to take your money out. The bottom line is you pay taxes on all your income.

W-2 vs. 1099 income

Most of your income will come from your job. You can get paid on a W-2 (standard employee) or 1099 (contractor). With W-2 income, your employer withholds your taxes and pays part of the employment taxes for you. With 1099 income, you are responsible for paying your own income taxes and will also have to pay self-employment taxes. The good thing about being paid on a 1099 is that you may have business deductions and may be eligible to open a Solo 401(k).

You probably won't have much of a choice on how you are paid. If you do gig work, that is going to be on a 1099. The same goes for selling items on eBay, most online transactions, and any time you receive over $600 via a cash app. There are a bunch of different types of 1099s, and you will also get one for any interest (1099-INT), dividends (1099-DIV), and retirement income (1099-R). Just remember that any money you get, you have to pay taxes on (unless exempted).

You pay income tax based on your filing status and the current tax brackets. The key to remember is that as your income goes up, you may end up in a new bracket, but that does not change the tax rate you pay on everything before that. Let me explain. In 2024, here is the tax table for a single person:

TAX RATE	TAXABLE INCOME BRACKET	TAX OWED
10%	$0 to $11,600	10% of taxable income
12%	$11,601 to $47,150	$1,160 Plus 12% of amount over $11,601

TAX RATE	TAXABLE INCOME BRACKET	TAX OWED
22%	$47,151 to $100,525	$5,426 Plus 22% of amount over $47,150
24%	$100,526 to $191,950	$17,168.50 Plus 24% of amount over $100,525
32%	$191,951 to $243,725	$39,110.50 Plus 32% of amount over $191,150
35%	$243,726 to $609,350	$55,678.50 Plus 35% of amount over $243,725
37%	$609,351 or more	$183,647.25 Plus 37% of amount over $609,350

This table can be super confusing, but here is what is important: If after the standard deduction your income is normally $40,000, you will pay 10% on the first $10,275, and 12% on the rest. Let's say you work some overtime in a year and make $45,000. Only what is over $41,775 will be charged the higher 22% rate. I point this out because I hear all the time that people don't want to make more money because it will "push them into a higher tax bracket." The facts are that the additional money will be taxed at the higher rate if you go into a new bracket, but it doesn't change anything before that. The bottom line is, go ahead and work that overtime if you want and pocket that extra cash. If your company offers bonuses, these will be taxed at a higher marginal rate, but it will all work out in the end.

DIVING DEEPER: For more, visit https://childfreewealth.com/42.

Disability income

One common area where you may not have to pay income taxes is on disability insurance income. This is true only if you paid for the policy yourself (and did not deduct it on your taxes). If your employer paid for it, and did not take taxes out, you will end up paying income taxes on your disability insurance income.

Lowering your modified adjusted gross income (MAGI) or adjusted gross income (AGI)

There are times you may want to lower your adjusted gross income (AGI) or modified adjusted gross income (MAGI). The IRS changes how they calculate AGI/MAGI over time, but the thing to remember is that it is the bottom line of how much the government says you made after tax credits or deductions. The most common time this happens is when you want to qualify for a government program, and particularly in the case of income-driven student loan payments. Using traditional 401(k)s, IRAs, and HSA accounts will all lower your gross income. Effectively, you get a tax break now in return for paying taxes later. HSAs are a little different in that contributions come out tax free for medical purposes.

The challenge with lowering your gross income now is that it builds up what can effectively be seen as a "tax debt." You haven't gotten out of paying taxes forever; you've just pushed them down the road. If you know your income will be lower in the future, then you can pay the taxes then (by doing a Roth conversion or taking out the income if you are over fifty-nine and a half years old). If on the other hand you expect your income to go up over your lifetime (as many do), then you may actually end up paying a higher rate in the future. The future is uncertain, so just be sure you know what the choices you make now are doing to your future taxes.

Capital gains tax

When you buy something (such as a stock), hold it for a while, and then sell it, you have entered the world of capital gains. If you hold it for a year or less, it is taxed as short-term capital gains(STCG). If you hold it for a year and one day, it is long-term capital gains (LTCG). Short-term capital gains end up at the same rates as income tax, but long-term capital gains are at the more favorable rates of 0%, 15%, or 20% (in 2024).

Yes, I did say LTCG could be at 0%. That only happens when your income is low for the year (below $47,025 for single people in 2024), but it is a window of opportunity to pay no taxes. Most people will fall into the 15% range, which is still below comparable income taxes in that range (22%–37% in 2024). So, whenever you can, you want to pay LTCG. You can control what is short- or long-term gains by how long you hold it. Additionally, if you receive qualified dividends, those are also taxed at LTCG rates. The bottom line is long-term, passive investing is designed to leverage LTCG rates.

Special cases for LTCG

There are two special cases to keep in mind when it comes to LTCG. Collectibles (such as coins and art) are taxed at a higher rate of 28%.

Your primary house is also special. If you have lived in the house for two out of the last five years, any gain up to $250K for a single person or $500K for married is tax free federally! Your home sale should be tax free in your state up to the same limit, but be sure to check. It is possible to get a partial tax break on your house if you have to move for certain reasons (such as a job change more than 50 miles away).

DIVING DEEPER: For more, visit https://childfreewealth.com/43.

Other federal taxes

The U.S. government has a series of other taxes beyond income and capital gains. You will pay taxes for Social Security and Medicare, and if your income is high enough, you will pay a net investment income tax of 3.8%. There is less you can do to impact those taxes, so I have chosen not to go deep into them. The one thing to watch out for is that in retirement, you may get assessed an income-related monthly adjustment amount (IRMAA) surcharge (they up your Medicare price) if you have too much income, but more on that in the section on planning healthcare in retirement.

State and local taxes

In addition to federal taxes, you may have to pay state, county, and even city taxes. Each state has its own combination of income taxes, sales taxes, and property taxes. The combination of these taxes can have a huge impact on your total tax bill. There are states that have no income taxes or no income taxes on retirement income, which can save you considerably in retirement. The problem is that states that have no income tax tend to have higher sales taxes. It becomes a complex math equation to decide which taxes you want to pay, and it depends on your income, lifestyle, and overall goals.

Property taxes can also vary widely. I had a $450K house in Connecticut, and my annual property taxes were $12,000. I bought a house in Mississippi for $440K, and my property taxes were $1,800. I had been so used to paying taxes in Connecticut that I thought the Mississippi taxes owed was a typo. Now, we can have a debate on what public services you get for those taxes, but the total amount is so different that it is shocking. As Childfree people and depending on our job situation, we can choose to live somewhere with lower taxes, which often coincides with a school district that's not as good, but that's okay for us. If you are a renter, you may not pay property taxes directly, but they are figured into your total rent cost by your landlord, so keep that in mind.

DIVING DEEPER: For more, visit https://childfreewealth.com/44.

OTHER TAX CONSIDERATIONS

The previous section outlined tax issues that most (nearing all) of you will run into. The next section outlines specific issues that are common, but you may not run into given your particular circumstances. Pick and choose which ones you read based upon your situation.

Roth conversions and backdoor Roths

Roth conversions and backdoor Roths are common areas people reach out to me about. The basic idea behind a Roth conversion is that you take money from a traditional IRA or 401(k), pay the taxes on it now, and then put it in your Roth IRA (so you never pay taxes on it again). The challenge with a Roth conversion is timing and tax rates. You want to do Roth conversions when your tax rates are at their lowest. For example, if you take an unpaid sabbatical and your income drops for the year, and you have extra money to pay the taxes, it may be a good time to do a Roth conversion. Same goes for early years of retirement before you claim Social Security and get hit by RMDs.

There is a bit more that goes into the decision to do a Roth conversion or not. When I look at a client's financial plans, my first debate is if they will end up using the Roth money or not. In retirement, the general rule is to take money from your taxable account first, then tax-deferred (traditional), and then finally tax-free (Roth). This order tends to result in the best tax effectiveness, as your tax-free money is allowed to grow as long as possible. Additionally, if you are giving money to family and friends, they would rather get the tax-free version. If you are using your Roth funds for your safety net, you may not want to add to them. If you are doing Roth conversions to avoid RMDs, you may be better off donating the money as QCDs. The bottom line is that if you do a Roth conversion now, you may be paying taxes on something that you could have avoided completely (by donating it).

If you do decide to do a Roth conversion, the best bet is to "fill up the bracket." What that means is that if you decide to do a Roth conversion and you are in the 22% tax bracket, convert enough to go right up to the top end of the bracket (just before it goes into 24%). If you are over sixty-five years old, you may end up going to the top of an IRMAA surcharge bracket to save on Medicare fees.

If it sounds complicated, it can be. The actual conversion itself is easy to do, as places like Vanguard have a system to do it, but the thought process can be a bit of a challenge. It is a good place to reach out to an advice-only or flat-fee CFP® professional.

The other place to reach out to a CFP® professional is if you are doing a backdoor Roth or mega backdoor Roth contribution. Here are the basics: Once you have gone over the Roth IRA income cap, you may still be able to make a backdoor Roth contribution. To do a backdoor Roth IRA contribution, you first make a non-deductible IRA contribution (which is reported to the IRS on an 8606 form), and then roll it into your Roth IRA. Sounds simple enough, but it only works perfectly if you have NO other traditional IRAs. If you have other traditional IRAs, you start having to worry about the IRS pro rata rules, and it becomes messy. I have spent so much time cleaning up backdoor Roths done wrong that I wonder if they are worth the hassle for most people. The mega backdoor Roth has similar mechanics but has to do with your 401(k), and it is only an option if your employer allows it. Get help in both cases.

DIVING DEEPER: For more, visit https://childfreewealth.com/35.

Running a small business and estimated taxes

If you get 1099 income, you are effectively running a small business. The IRS does not care if you have an actual business (like an LLC), do gig work, or consulting— it is all treated as a small business. The IRS sees an LLC (limited liability company) as a "disregarded entity," which in plain language means they just see it as you. No matter the structure, you are responsible for not only filing your own taxes but also paying estimated taxes. As a small business owner, you have to do your own tax withholding. In addition to your standard income taxes, you need to pay a self-employment tax of 15.3%. Self-employment tax covers 12.4% for Social Security and 2.9% for Medicare.

What can be confusing is that you pay taxes on your *net* income. Net income is what is left over after you pay all your business expenses. Note, I said *business* expenses. Be very careful to not mix business and personal expenses. I recommend that all small business owners read the book *Profit First*, and it will get you started with a basic bookkeeping/accounting system. The bottom line is that you need to know your numbers and plan for taxes.

DIVING DEEPER: For more, visit https://childfreewealth.com/48.

Gifting and other tax issues for unmarried couples

If you are married, there is an unlimited gifting exemption. What that means is that you can give your spouse as much money as you want. This is because as a married couple you file your taxes together (even if you file married filing separately) and the IRS doesn't care much about who has what, as it is all the same to them.

The rules are completely different for a couple who are not married (or a group for that matter). When you are not married, the IRS treats any gifts as they would a gift to anyone else. The IRS has an annual gift limit ($18,000 in 2024) for each person. You can give someone money, up to the limit, without having to pay taxes on it. If you go over the limit, you may be able to use your gift and estate tax exemption ($13.61 million in 2024), but you do need to file for that exemption. The estate tax exemption is there for passing on wealth at death and is slated to go down in 2025 (to approximately $5.49 million), so when you use it matters. If you go over the estate exemption, the tax rate can be up to 40%.

Let's look at some examples of how this can impact you:

You buy your partner a car. You're not married. The car costs $50,000. The car is over the limit. You could use $18,000 of your annual gift limit, but you then need to use your estate exemption for the remaining $32,000.

You are part of an unmarried group and give all four members of your group $10,000 each (a total of $40,000). Nothing to file here, as each person received less than $18,000.

You buy a house and pass it to your partner in your estate. The value of the house needs to be claimed against your estate exemption.

If it sounds sticky, it's because it is. The only thing you can do is to keep track and file taxes appropriately. You may look at the $13.61 million limit and assume you will never hit it, but over your lifetime, it is much easier than it seems. Each time you claim against it, it lowers the amount you can pass in your estate (yet another good reason to wind down your wealth).

In addition to gifting issues, a married couple can exclude up to $500,000 in capital gains when they sell their primary residence, as long as they have lived there for two of the last five years. A single person can only exclude $250,000. Depending on how you own the home together (i.e., if you both have your names on it and both live there for two years), it will change how much you can each exclude from the sale.

Employee stock options

If your employer offers you stock options—incentive stock options (ISOs) or the like—or restricted stock units (RSUs) as part of your compensation package, it can cause some tax challenges. When and how you execute the stock purchases and sales will change how and when you are taxed. In even a small equity stake, it can be a very large tax bill. There are entire books written on this topic, so I'm not going to try to give you an answer here. Just know that if you have equity compensation you need to work with a CFP® professional and a CPA to determine the best option for you. Don't go it alone.

DIVING DEEPER: For more, visit https://childfreewealth.com/94.

Other taxes

Depending on your situation, you may have additional city, county, state, or federal taxes you must pay. The more complex your finances are, the more complex your taxes can be. If you live or work in multiple states, you may have multiple taxes that need to be paid. When in doubt, contact a professional. You are responsible for knowing what taxes you need to pay, and ignorance is not a valid excuse.

18
BUYING A HOUSE (OR NOT)

What do you want your retirement to look like?

"Owning a fully paid house (to be safe from rising rents and loss of income), having enough passive income to pay the bills, and have some extra at the end of the month."

—SARA, TWENTY-SEVEN, MARRIED

Buying a house is a choice for Childfree people, not a requirement. It flies in the face of standard financial advice, but there are other ways to get exposure to real estate as an investment that may be better than buying a house. Buying a house is part of the standard life plan, and there is a lot of pressure on people to buy. Don't get sucked into house fever.

Renting is not evil or throwing money away, no matter how many people tell you otherwise. The bonus of renting is that you have flexibility and less financial responsibility. If you are renting and your hot water heater goes out, you call maintenance. If you own your home and the hot water heater blows, it is your problem. It also costs 6% or more to sell a house, and depending on the market it may take time. With renting, you can move whenever you want and only pay extra if you break your lease.

I'm going to run you through an extensive list of questions and thoughts to consider before you buy a house. Go through each of them, think about your answer, and if you still want to buy a house at the end, I'll give you some guidelines later.

If the mortgage is the same amount as the rent, shouldn't I buy? Rent represents the maximum you will owe each month for your housing. A mortgage payment is the minimum you will have to pay. In addition to the mortgage, you need to pay for property tax, insurance, maintenance, upkeep, and repairs. On average you will spend 1% of your home's value each year on maintenance. The problem is that maintenance/repairs are "lumpy," not a standard monthly amount. If you need to replace your roof or HVAC, you are looking at more than $10K. In other years, you may have very little maintenance besides some painting. The unpredictability of repairs can be a challenge to budget for. Additionally, you need to either do the work yourself or hire someone to do all the work associated with the house. While you might enjoy mowing the lawn the first time it is yours, remember you also need to mow it in the hot, humid days of summer and when the pollen count is through the roof.

Can't I buy a house and then rent it out later (or other versions of house hacking)? You can rent out your house in some cases. Keep in mind that some communities (or HOAs) have laws against short-term rentals (Airbnb and the like). The problem is that the house you would buy as an investment to rent out is often different from the house you would buy to live in. If you are buying an investment property, you will tend to do better with a multifamily unit than a single-family home. Also, if you ever move to another state, remote land lording is not a great idea. If you plan on paying someone to manage the property for you, you might as well just invest in a real estate investment trust (REIT).

If I don't buy a house now, I may never be able to afford one. The reality is that you may never be able to afford to buy a house, and that is okay. Housing prices in the United States have been rising at astronomical rates when compared to incomes. We have a mounting housing crisis. As I write this book, mortgage rates are on the rise and house prices are also. In most major metropolitan areas, even though it is expensive to rent, it is still cheaper to rent than to buy, and that is okay. Don't let FOMO or the pressure of the "great American dream" force you into a house purchase.

But I need a house if I want to retire. Okay, our grandparents bought a house, lived in it their whole life, paid it off, and retired with no house payment. If you can do that, great! On average, people live in their house for eight years before they move.[9] If you are in your thirties or forties, that means you may move three or more times before you retire. When people move, they tend to buy bigger and more expensive homes. The bottom line is that we are not like our grandparents, and the likelihood of the next house you buy being your "forever home" is low. The average stat I mentioned is in the entire population, and Childfree people tend to be more mobile. I can't find good data, but my guess is that our average years spent in one house will be lower.

But I don't want to live in an apartment anymore; I want a yard for my dog and a garden. Apartment living has its challenges. Before you buy a house in order to have a garden (or whatever other project you want), think about renting a house. It is possible to rent a house and get the benefits you are looking for. Don't equate the false dichotomy choice of apartment versus house to be the same as rent versus buy.

But I want to settle down. Cool, then settle down. You don't have to move every two years if you do not want to. You can settle

9 "Average Length of Homeownership: Americans Spend Less than 15 Years in One Home," The Zebra, September 7, 2023, https://www.thezebra.com/resources/home/average-length-of-homeownership/.

down in a long-term rental just as you can a house you buy. You still have a risk that your landlord will sell the home or kick you out, but you can try to get a long-term lease to protect yourself.

But rents keep going up. True. So do mortgages. As your home value goes up, so do your property taxes (and potentially homeowners' insurance) so your monthly payment will go up. Also, the longer you own a house, the higher the likelihood that you will need to do a big, expensive maintenance project.

But I can write off the mortgage interest. True, kinda. Most people in the United States take the standard deduction, which means they are not itemizing and getting the break on mortgage interest. There is also a cap on mortgage interest deductibility.

But I want to paint my walls and do home projects. Okay, you got me here. If your passion is in doing home projects, you may need to buy a house. My wife and I redid an 1880s house. It was fun learning how to reglaze windows (for the first two windows—don't ask about the other twenty). If your passion is in home repair and maintenance, then either buy a house or start a handyman business.

I could keep going, but I think you get the point. The decision to buy or rent is not as simple as comparing your rent to a mortgage payment. I will say that if you don't see yourself staying in the house for five to seven years (or more), renting is likely to be the right choice.

ARE YOU READY TO BUY A HOUSE?

If you decide you want to buy a house, you are ready when you meet the following four conditions:

1. You are completely out of debt.
2. You have a six-month emergency fund.
3. You have 20% to put down on the house (on top of your emergency fund).
4. Your mortgage payment (including principal, interest, taxes, and insurance) is less than one-third of your take-home pay.

To be clear, you can qualify for a home mortgage with debt, a smaller down payment, and with a higher monthly payment, but just because you *can* does not mean you *should*. I'm trying to prevent you from being house poor. When you are house poor, you end up putting everything you have into the house and do not have enough money left over to live.

You want to be out of debt and have a fully funded emergency fund so that you can handle emergencies with the house. When you have no debt and a six-month emergency fund, you can just write a check and turn most emergencies into inconveniences. Just remember to refill your emergency fund ASAP. For example, at my last house we had a lightning strike near the house. We ended up having four electrician visits and two by our generator maintenance person, resulting in a bill of about $5K. We had the funds to handle it, but if you can't figure out how to pay for the electrician to get your power back, that is going to be a tough time.

I recommend putting down 20% on your house both to avoid private mortgage insurance (PMI) and to ensure you can get out if needed. You can buy a house with as little down as 3.5% with a Federal Housing Administration (FHA) loan. The challenge is that if you buy a house with that little down, you start off underwater and can't sell the house without bringing money to the closing table (it costs 6%+ to sell). PMI is insurance you pay for to protect the lender and has no value to you.

PMI is paid upfront or monthly, both raising your total cost, so avoid it if at all possible.

My goal is for your housing payment to be less than one-third of your take-home income. Keep in mind that when mortgage brokers are looking at payments when determining how much you qualify for, their goal is 28% to 31% of your gross income (before taxes). There is a huge difference between 33% of your take-home and 31% of your gross for many people. I know that in some high-cost-of-living areas, it may be nearly impossible to keep your housing cost below one-third of your take-home pay. If you are going to pay more, it is going to make your budget tight, and you will have to make choices about what is important.

DIVING DEEPER: For more, visit https://childfreewealth.com/16.

INVESTING IN REAL ESTATE WITHOUT BUYING A HOUSE

If you don't buy a property, you can still get the benefits of owning real estate by buying REITs. The bonus with buying a REIT is that you are effectively buying into a variety of properties and a management company is managing them for you. With REITs, they are required to pay 90% of their taxable income back each year as a dividend. If you want to think about this as rental income, close enough.

The bonus of buying REITs is that you can buy into a wide variety of properties. You aren't limited to buying single-family homes. You can buy into commercial properties, hospitals, self-storage facilities, and just about any type of real estate you can think of. If you follow our three-fund portfolio recommendation, you are already investing in REITs. Approximately 3% to 4% of VTI and VXUS is invested in publicly traded REITs. If you want more real estate exposure, you can look at Vanguard's Real Estate Fund (VNQ) or other similar funds, but just realize these will throw off income, which may be good or bad for your taxes.

DIVING DEEPER: For more, visit https://childfreewealth.com/19.

A SPECIAL NOTE ABOUT MORTGAGES, LEVERAGE, TEN-TIMES, AND OTHER REAL ESTATE IDEAS

If you are on the internet at all, you've probably seen someone selling a course or structure to buy real estate, sometimes with no money down, as an investment. It is probably no surprise that I'm not a fan of the Grant Cardones of the world trying to ten-times your money with debt. While it is possible to make money in real estate this way, it is also risky. If you really want to buy physical real estate properties as an investment, consider buying them with cash (then you can keep all the rent). If you are not willing to put your own money into buying a property, why would you borrow someone else's money to put into it?

The bottom line is to make sure you differentiate between real estate to live in and as an investment. If you are looking for a place to live in, make sure it matches your life and finances. You don't have to buy a house just out of FOMO or because someone else says you have to.

19

RUNNING A SMALL BUSINESS AND SIDE GIGS

What do you want your retirement to look like?

"Ideally, retirement would consist of traveling, spending time with family, and pursuing passion projects. These passion projects may be paid work (most likely self-employment), but work that I believe in, that gives my retirement and existence a purpose—probably helping cats!"

—JAVIER, THIRTY-FOUR, MARRIED

So many Childfree people run a small business or have a side gig that I decided to dedicate a chapter to the ups and downs of entrepreneurship. If you have ever debated starting a business or dream of one day owning your own job (i.e., being a solopreneur or being your own boss), read on. It is one of the more rewarding things you can do with your life, but it can also be much more stressful. I enjoy running my own business and learned years ago that I'm better being my own boss. That being said, I'm hard on myself, always push myself, and am working on my own balance, so you should know what you are signing up for.

I've owned a variety of businesses across my life. My parents love to tell the story about my first business, selling pinecones. My grandfather sold Christmas trees when I was growing up, and I set up a stand at his place collecting and selling pinecones. The pricing was simple, 1¢ if the customer picked up the pinecones from the ground, and 5¢ if I picked them up for them. (At least it proves I knew the cost of labor even when I was very young. I'm not sure how you scale a pinecone business charging $0.05 a piece, but I did make money.)

The core questions when it comes to running a business are simple: Who do you want to serve, and how do you want to serve them? Once you have the answers to those questions, the challenge then becomes actually making a profit (or breaking even at least).

Let me show you how this works in practice by dissecting my business, Childfree Wealth®, as an example. To understand me, how I work, and any business I run, you first need to know the two mantras/sayings that have guided my entire life:

> "You can have everything in life you want if you just help enough other people get what they want."—Zig Ziglar
>
> "Work smarter, not harder."—Scrooge McDuck

Yes, I did just quote Scrooge McDuck. If you don't know who that is, it is a cartoon character from comic books and the TV show *Duck Tales*. He is a fictional character that is the richest duck in the world (and Donald Duck's uncle, for the Disney fans). If you think about the pinecone example, that is a perfect example of work smarter, not harder. The point is not to grind and sweat but to optimize what you do for the biggest return on investment with the least work. If your business relies on you always working hard, it is not sustainable.

Zig, on the other hand, is talking about a mindset of service. If you see any of my emails, they are signed "yours in service" and always have been. It is archaic, but it is the way I look at the world. My focus is on serving others and helping in any way possible. The key to Zig's philosophy is that there is the hope that at some point, serving others will help you. It puts others first, but so that you can have everything in life that you want.

With Zig and Scrooge in mind, I created Childfree Wealth®, answering these two questions as follows.

Whom do I want to serve? Childfree and Permanently Childless people in the United States. Besides being Childfree myself, I see Childfree people as an underserved and underrepresented group in the financial world. It is a large group, but when I started my firm, there was no one else dedicated to serving Childfree people, and the idea of Childfree financial planning was nearly non-existent.

How do I want to serve them? My PhD is in adult learning and I LOVE helping people to learn. I want to help Childfree people learn how to manage their finances and make their finances boring so that their life can be AMAZING! I don't want them to always have to rely on me; I want them to graduate at some point and come back only if they need help.

There are tons of books on starting businesses out there, but if you can figure out both who you want to serve and how, you have done the hardest part of business planning. If you know both who and how, creating products that meet those needs, marketing to that group, and getting sales will all grow out of your core answers. I freely admit that I've redesigned my products/pricing dozens of times and rebuilt my website almost monthly, but who and how I serve have not changed. Your answers to those two questions will serve as a true north to keep you moving, focused on what matters and working toward profitability.

With your true north in place, the next step is to create a minimum viable product (MVP). Note, I didn't say that your next step is to make a fifty-page business plan. We can get stuck in analysis paralysis if we focus too much on getting the business plan "right" before launching. You need to get your MVP out there and get feedback. Start small, start with cash (not a business loan), and just get started. You will learn more from customer feedback than reading any book or building any plan. If you really need to read business books, read *The Lean Startup* and *Profit First.*

A note about legalese: Childfree Wealth® is a Registered Investment Advisor (RIA) with the Securities and Exchange Commission (SEC). Forming an RIA is a considerable undertaking with considerable costs and compliance requirements, so it was a big endeavor. Each company has its own requirements, so it's imperative that you figure out what rules you need to follow for your business. Some states and industries have very little regulation. On the other hand, when I was selling firewood in front of my house in Connecticut, I needed multiple permits just to put out a stand and an honor box to collect cash. Make sure you know your own rules.

With the legalese handled, and an MVP, it is time to try things. It is very rare for your first idea to be perfect. The key is to get feedback, make improvements, and move forward. If you can't accept feedback, owning a business may not be right for you. The challenge is to be able to sort through all the feedback you get to find the gold in there, rather than just the hate.

From the start of Childfree Wealth®, I've had haters. I'm amazed by the number of people who are "praying for my Childless soul." I'll admit that early on, the hate hurt, and I needed a thicker skin. Now, I treat it like a video game: if you run into enemies, you are running in the right direction.

With a product and feedback, it is time to finally do some real business planning. You can use tools like a Business Model Canvas to get your ideas out there. Combine that with the principles from the book *Profit First* and you will be able to model out a profitable business. If your current product (after feedback) isn't going to be profitable, it may be time to go back and try a different product or pricing.

Just make sure you are not only making a profit but that you are paying yourself for your time. For any new business, I employ the McDonald's test that I mentioned earlier: If you can make more per hour working at McDonald's than running your own business, you may want to work at McDonald's. There will always be growth phases where you make less. You may also choose to set up a nonprofit, which is fine. But the key is that you need a return on your investment. There are non-monetary returns on investment also, but that is for people who are in No-Baby Step 8.

With most businesses, your first year or two will be the hardest. You may make little or no money. To this end, I encourage people to start their business as a side gig while working their full-time job. It is tough to run a business and work forty hours at another full-time job, but it gives you a safety net while you learn the ups and downs of running a business and to improve your product. Once your business is making enough for you to live on, you can quit your day job.

Keep in mind that as a business owner, you need to learn both how to provide a good product or service and how to run the business itself. I regularly find people who are really good at serving customers but not so great at running a business. You can be the best cupcake baker in the world, but if you can't run the financial or customer-facing sides of the business you may never make it. You know yourself best, so be honest about where you need to improve. Running a small business is a skill in itself. I regularly help people learn how to optimize their business, and I don't need to know much at all about how to bake a cupcake to help them.

As your business grows, you need to enlist help. It might be a business coach, a CFP® professional, a CPA, a mastermind group, or any combination of people who can best help you. Right now, for my business, I have hired coaches for specific topics (most recently on public relations), and I am a member of three mastermind groups, which are places for people with a common business to get together and share ideas. I learn something from just about every mastermind meeting I'm in and try to never skip them. Find your group and your people to grow.

DIVING DEEPER: For more, visit https://childfreewealth.com/57.

SEPARATE BUSINESS AND PERSONAL FINANCES

One caution on running a small business: keep your personal and business finances separate. You need a financial plan for yourself and one for your business, and they should not be mixed together. Many entrepreneurs, especially if you are the only employee, smush together their personal and business finances. ("Smush" isn't a technical term, but you get my point.) Your business needs its own budget, emergency fund, investments, and more. You don't want a bad month in the business to bury you personally.

If you do nothing else, keep separate accounts for your business and personal expenses. Just because you can charge it to the business does not mean it is a valid expense to the IRS. Your business account (or accounts if you follow the *Profit First* method) should take in all business income and pay all business expenses. You should then pay yourself from the business, either as an employee or as an owner.

Keeping separate accounts will also help protect you against liability. If you create an LLC (limited liability company/corporation), it can protect you from liability, but if you mix your personal and professional expenses you may have "pierced the veil" of the LLC. (That is a fancy way of saying that if you don't treat your company as a separate entity, the courts may also treat them as one and the same.)

If you have ever thought about starting your own business, you probably should. It may be a success, or not, but you probably need to give it a shot. It is not as easy as you see on *Shark Tank*, but it can be fun.

DIVING DEEPER: For more, visit https://childfreewealth.com/58.

20

WHY THE 4% RULE IS WRONG FOR CHILDFREE FOLKS

What do you want your retirement to look like?

"I need to feel productive in retirement, so it won't be a non-working thing for me. I will continue to be entrepreneurial and hope to be able to enter the wine industry. I know for certain that I do not want to stay in the construction industry. My husband and I want to live internationally. Travel will be a big part of my retirement. To be able to live without monetary concerns is an ideal retirement for me."

—CHARLIE, THIRTY-FOUR, MARRIED

The 4% safe withdrawal rate (SWR) rule is so popular in the Financial Independence, Retire Early (FIRE) world that it needs a discussion here. Originally created by Bill Bengen in the nineties, it has grown in popularity as back-of-the-napkin math to calculate how much money you need to retire. The basic question it answers is how much money can you safely take out each year in retirement (over thirty years) and have a low likelihood of running out of money. There has been considerable research since then that challenges the 4% number, with some suggesting 3%, others 5%, but most of the debate is around which period of time you are looking at for a baseline. I'm going to use 4% as a discussion point here.

What is nice about the SWR of 4%, is that it gives you a goal. The basic concept is that if you have a $2 million net worth, you can take out $80K each year (adjusted for inflation) and have a low likelihood of running out of money. The inverse of the rule says that if you take your annual expenses and multiply them by 25, it will tell you how much you need to have saved for retirement (i.e., if you have $40K in expenses, you need $1 million to retire). As with any simple rule, there are caveats and challenges. For Childfree people, we have two giant problems with the SWR: (1) We may not want to retire and live the Financial Independence, Live Early (FILE) lifestyle instead, and (2) we may want to die with zero.

If your goal is to embrace the FILE lifestyle, you are likely to have some money coming in across your life and won't have a thirty-year retirement. People following FILE end up investing in themselves and their lives in different ways that are not accounted for by the SWR. If you want to hit your FI number (25 times your expenses) and then cut back work, that is fine, but you are likely to have too much money left over. Additionally, the SWR assumes you want to preserve your principal, which means there is a very low likelihood of dying with zero, which goes against your goals.

In practice, I use the 4% SWR as a discussion point. I don't debate the exact percentage but use it as a measure of when clients need to start bending their net worth curve. If you are going to spend your money during your lifetime, you need to spend more than you make, which can be challenging for some (the blueberry problem I mentioned earlier). It doesn't matter much at what age you hit your FI number; the key is that at some point you need to make sure your finances are going toward your goals.

MOVING THE GOALPOSTS

The danger is that once someone hits their FI number, they will move the goalposts. If your goal is to have $2 million to retire, once you hit that goal, all too many people change the number to $4 million (or some other goal). I've heard all versions of this including:

> Well, $2 million wasn't that hard, so I might as well try for more.
>
> Two million dollars doesn't go as far as it used to.
>
> What if inflation continues, Social Security collapses, etc....
>
> I'm not ready to retire...

The bottom line for most people is that it can be scary figuring out what to do next. If you have spent decades of your life working toward your goal, you might feel much like the dog that caught the car... Now what are you supposed to do?

The problem for Childfree people is that each dollar you earn beyond your goal is going to an estate that is not your priority. If your net worth gets high enough, you may actually be working to give the U.S. government 40% in estate taxes, which no one really wants to do. If your net worth is invested appropriately, it will grow on its own. When you've hit your FI number, chances are you hit the "tipping point" when you are making more off your investments than your salary. The bottom line is that even if you don't move the goalposts, your net worth will continue to grow unless you do something about it.

I will freely admit that getting clients to stop moving the goalposts is a challenge. I will do their entire financial plan for them, show them the math, and they will still fight me. They will ask me dozens of what-ifs, question my assumptions, returns, and more. I meet with clients monthly, and it usually takes around three months for them to accept that they are set financially. Once they finally agree that they have hit their goal, the Childfree Midlife Crisis truly sets in... What next?

For truly goal-driven people, I have found the best thing is to just give them another goal. I'm not going to try to reprogram their inherent drives and motivations. I tend to do a lot of visioning work with them to find another goal that can be just as rewarding as increasing their net worth. It becomes a shift from money to impact for many. Some people start a small business or a nonprofit to follow their passions. Others go back to school, change careers completely, and start over. Yet others set lofty travel goals and work on ticking off their bucket list. It really doesn't matter what your goals are, but you are better off switching to a new goal than just mindlessly moving the goalposts.

SETTING UP GUARDRAILS FOR SPENDING

If you want to get your numbers dialed in perfectly, and not rely on the SWR of 4%, this is a great place to work with a CERTIFIED FINANCIAL PLANNER™. This professional can look at your numbers unemotionally, which tends to be more important than the math itself (software does the real math). When reviewing their own numbers, people tend to do too much "mental accounting." In mental accounting, we end up with buckets of money (i.e., travel money versus expenses), which can prevent us from looking at the big picture and will get in the way of the core question, which is: How much do I have to spend (or give) in order to die with zero?

The best solution is to set up guardrails for your spending. In a guardrails approach, you don't use an SWR, but you have a minimum and maximum spending goal. For example, your spending goal might be a minimum of $150,000 per year, plus half of the market gain from last year (which serves as the maximum). Each person's guardrails will be different and will reflect their goals, net worth, taxes, and spending habits (especially impacted by giving to charities).

In most cases, I find that clients are spending nowhere near what they need to in order to spend down their net worth. Spending that much goes against all the behaviors they built to get them to that point. That is why I like to implement a minimum spending goal. The SWR reflects a maximum withdrawal rate, so it is an inverse way of thinking. To make spending more palatable, I will often try to connect a spending goal to a giving goal (e.g., give away as much money as you spend on travel for the year).

Your guardrails will need to be tweaked across your life. It isn't a one-and-done type of thing. The problem is that the stock market returns a *lifetime* average of 7% to 10%, not every year. There is a risk in all retirement plans called the *sequence of returns risk* (SOR). The basics are that if your first few years in retirement (or embracing FILE) are great years for the market, you are likely to have a lot of money left if you leave your guardrails where they are. This is why I like setting guardrails as a minimum plus a percentage of return. In down years, you will have only the minimum, but in up years you will have to work harder to spend.

Your taxes and retirement accounts will have a huge impact on the real math. If you have saved everything in Roth accounts, it is pretty easy, but most people have a combination of taxable, tax-deferred, and tax-free accounts. As you stop working, you may want to consider doing Roth conversions in lower tax years both to benefit from the long-term tax savings but also to avoid required minimum distributions (RMDs). If you are going to be giving regularly to charities, you will be better off giving away your taxable and tax-deferred money. You can give away from your traditional IRAs/401(k) as qualified charitable distributions (QCDs) when you are over seventy and a half years old. The bottom line with taxes is that you need a plan for which money to use and when over the remainder of your life to lower your taxes. The problem is that tax laws change all the time. What was a good plan one year can be completely flipped by a new tax law the next year.

The best answer is to do a check-in each year with your CFP® professional and CPA to make any adjustments for the next year. You can do all your own investments and don't need to pay them to manage your investments, but you need a tune-up here and there to make sure you are on the right track.

DIVING DEEPER: For more, visit https://childfreewealth.com/100.

21
THE BORING MIDDLE

What are your goals?

"Originally, I had financial goals. I wanted to have a million dollars by the time I was fifty. I did it at thirty-four. I grew up very poor and with a terrible family. I never thought I would have such a perfect-for-me life. At this point, I just need to coast and sustain."

—GALE, THIRTY-SIX, MARRIED

There is a spot in between conquering the No-Baby Steps and reaching financial independence called the "boring middle" that you need to be aware of. It is where people tend to make mistakes. Here's how it works: You create a financial plan, pay off your debt, and are now working on increasing your net worth. You are on a path to financial independence, and all you have to do is keep to the plan and wait. It may be years or decades before you hit your goal, but you will as long as you keep to the plan. The problem is that the boredom in this spot tends to cause people to do stupid things.

Getting out of debt is a challenge, and you get positive reinforcement each time you pay off a debt. The challenge and rewards keep you motivated. You can watch your net worth grow from negative numbers to zero and celebrate. Once you get out of debt and have a fully funded emergency fund, you will be close to $100K in net worth. Getting to $100K is also something to celebrate. Getting to $1 million from $100K is just a matter of time if you keep doing what got you there. From $1 million to whatever goal you have, it is purely a matter of time.

When people get into the boring middle, they tend to start tinkering. They may want to look at alternative investments or use other tools to increase their earnings. Or they might want to start dabbling in buying individual stocks or the next hot tip they got from their friend. Really, they are looking for the adrenaline rush that comes from the ups and downs. If you start tinkering with the plan that got you to this point, you may not get to your goals in the end.

As Jack Bogle, founder of Vanguard, famously said, "Don't do something—just stand there!" The plan I laid out in this book is based around much of Bogle's work and passive investing as a whole. The point is to invest your money, let it work for you, and not change anything unless there is a major shift. What counts as a major shift? In the stock market, there is very little that can occur that I would consider a major shift. More likely you may have a major shift in your goals or life that may cause you to reevaluate your financial plan. If that is the case, you adjust your overall plan; you don't change the principles that it is based upon. A major shift is not a reason to start doing silly things with your investments.

So how do you manage the boredom? Live an amazing life! My goal is for you to check your financial plan and net worth twice a year. The challenge is to stop thinking about your investments and focus on the life you want to live. If you need an adrenaline boost, get it from your life. Challenge yourself elsewhere and let the plan work its way through.

A last caution: watch out for drama. If you have been living in fear and anxiety around your money most of your life, you may inadvertently create drama to stay in fear. Your body is used to living in anxiety and may subconsciously be looking for it. I've seen people get stir-crazy and make up a reason they have to make a drastic change (think job change, house change, life change). It is not always visible when you are the one creating the drama, so make sure you have an accountability partner to help you keep things boring.

22
SOCIAL SECURITY

What does Childfree Wealth mean to you?

"It means you have what you need and maybe a bit more. It means you can splurge on yourself now and again without wondering if it will break the bank. It means being comfortable in your own skin. You are living for you and not for other people."

—NADIA, THIRTY-SEVEN, SINGLE

Up until now, I've been focused on you saving for your own retirement or Financial Independence, Live Early (FILE) lifestyle. That is intentional. My goal is for you to look at Social Security as a bonus, not as a tool to rely on for income when you are older. My recommendation to most people is to put off collecting Social Security until age seventy (as part of their die-with-zero plan), as it is when you get the largest payment. The problem is that there is no guarantee that you will get anything. The current estimate is that in 2033 Social Security will run out of money and need to pay about 77% of covered benefits. What that means is that if you were expecting to get $1,000 in benefits, you will instead get $770. I hope it will be fixed by then, but I am not counting on it personally.

It may be helpful to review what Social Security is (and isn't) to help this make sense. The technical term for Social Security is the Old-Age, Survivors and Disability Insurance (OASDI) program. You may have seen OASDI on your pay stub, and that is money going to Social

Security. Social Security provides an income in retirement or when you're disabled. The good thing is that Social Security payments are adjusted for cost of living, but for many people these payments may not be enough to live on.

The challenge is that Social Security is a bit of a pyramid scheme (technically it is not a pyramid scheme, as there is no intent to fraud, but it works much the same way). The money you pay into Social Security today goes to pay benefits for other people today. There is not an account with your money in it waiting for you (like an IRA), just an IOU from the government. The problem with a pyramid scheme is that it requires constant growth to stay solvent. Decreasing birth rates and population growth have the potential to collapse Social Security.

Rant INCOMING! When I talk about being Childfree in the finance arenas, I often get pushback that we need more kids to pay for social programs, including Social Security. They are correct that the system requires constant growth, but that is a flaw in the system, not in Childfree people choosing not to have kids. Constant growth is not good for our environment, but our economy requires it to maintain the current trajectory. The system is broken, and the solution is NOT to say that Childfree or Childless people are the problem. **Rant over.**

Since I think the system is broken, I don't want people to rely on it. In my own personal financial plan, I assume that I will get 75% of what Social Security says my payment will be (I'll be seventy in 2048, well past when it runs out of money). I don't think it is reasonable to assume that there will be no Social Security payments, as that would result in near societal collapse in the United States. That being said, I'm watching closely what Japan does, as they are currently having huge population shifts and have a higher Childfree population, so it may give us clues on how to handle things.

If you really think you will get nothing from Social Security, the answer is to have a bit larger of a cash cushion in your die-with-zero plan. Keep in mind that if you think Social Security is truly at risk, you may want to consider that Medicare and Medicaid won't be there either in your retirement plan.

DIVING DEEPER: For more, visit https://childfreewealth.com/101.

23

HEALTHCARE AND MEDICARE IN RETIREMENT

What does Childfree Wealth mean to you?

"A comfortable lifestyle in adulthood (i.e., no strict budget, new hobbies can be picked up, travel, etc., within reason) while saving heavily for retirement. My goal is to have at least five million dollars for retirement, preferably ten million since I want to retire early. Heavy investment in long-term care insurance as well."

—JOSEPHINE, TWENTY-TWO, SINGLE

Healthcare is one of the most common reasons why I hear people putting off embracing the Financial Independence, Live Early (FILE) lifestyle or retirement. The cost of healthcare in retirement has become a bit of a boogeyman for many. While it is expensive, it is a cost that can be planned for. For simple math, I plan on $25K per year for healthcare for a couple (half for soloists). You need to plan on paying for healthcare at least until Medicare kicks in at sixty-five, and then you need to just cover out-of-pocket costs. That number is probably high in most cases but reflects both monthly premiums and out-of-pocket costs. The real number is likely to be lower. Most states have a healthcare marketplace with a tax break for lower incomes. If you are completely retired and not working, your income may be low enough to qualify for a tax break and lower your healthcare costs.

When shopping for a plan on the marketplace, I usually recommend a gold or platinum plan. Gold and platinum plans tend to have the best coverage and lowest out-of-pocket costs. If you go with a bronze or silver plan, you will lower your monthly costs but will be responsible for a higher deductible and maximum out-of-pocket amount. With healthcare, I tend to overinsure a bit and go with the better plan unless you are young and in near perfect health. I will jokingly ask if people are "lucky." If you are prone to bad luck, cheaping out on healthcare premiums can bite you in the end.

MEDICARE

When you hit sixty-five, you will most likely qualify for Medicare. Even if you are still working at sixty-five, you may want to enroll in Medicare. You will get a notice three months before your sixty-fifth birthday, and it is important to enroll on time. Medicare is made up of three parts:

Part A: Hospital insurance. Think of Part A as covering in patient care or bills paid to the hospital.

Part B: Medical insurance. Think of Part B as covering your primary care doctors or bills paid to a doctor's office.

Part D: Prescription drugs. Think of Part D as paying for prescribed drugs from a pharmacy.

There are a variety of plan choices for Medicare. The challenge is to find the right one for you. You may want to contact your local social worker or Medicare consultant to find the right fit. It can be confusing, but you need to make your choices on time.

From a financial standpoint, once you are on Medicare you need to watch out for income-related monthly adjustment amount (IRMAA) surcharges. As your income goes up, so does the amount you are charged for Medicare parts B and D. You will pay an additional amount each month, but there is effectively a two-year lag in IRMAA charges (i.e., your taxes in 2023 impact your IRMAA surcharge in 2025). The ranges change each year, but it can be easy to hit a $500 to $600/month IRMAA surcharge if you don't plan your income taxes.

When you create your deaccumulation plan, you need a plan for IRMAA. For example, doing a Roth conversion will increase your taxable income (and IRMAA surcharge), while taking a distribution from a Roth account is tax free and will not impact your IRMAA. People usually learn about IRMAA after they get hit with it. For example, if you sell a bunch of stock from your taxable account to pay for your new boat, and you are sixty-five, IRMAA is going to hit you two years later, so you need to be smart about your income.

With all of that said, IRMAA surcharges are not a reason to cut back on your life. If you need the income to make yourself happy or reach your goals, you just need to plan for the increased monthly expense.

DIVING DEEPER: For more, visit https://childfreewealth.com/96.

24
MONEY BEHAVIORS

What does Childfree Wealth mean to you?

"My money is my own. My independence is a hard-fought-for struggle that I earned. I get to enjoy it for myself. I can be as selfish as I want with my money."

—ROSEMARY, THIRTY, MARRIED

While it is hard to exactly quantify, the general rule with finance is that 80% of your success is related to your money behaviors, and 20% on the actual numbers. Sure, if you are in the rent-and-ramen phase and can barely pay your bills, it is probably more about the actual numbers. Once you get past paying for basic needs, it truly is about your own behaviors.

I'm going to get a bit nerdy here and pull out some of the work from my PhD, so be forewarned. Our money behaviors are created by a combination of our own individual beliefs (or mental models), our experiences, and our money environment. In order to change your money behaviors, you need to be aware of your current mental models (or way of thinking) and challenge them with a new (hopefully improved) mental model. The problem is that most of our behaviors and mental models are tacit or subconscious, so changing them can be a challenge. We tend to change our mental models (learn) when we try a new model on a new experience, in a supportive environment.

Throughout this book I have focused on shifting your mental models around money. I have given you a series of mental models to try out to plan and improve your money behaviors. To make it clear, here are the major mental models to consider:

Plan your life, then your finances.

Ditch the Standard LifeScript and make your own.

Financial Independence, FILE, and FIRE are possible.

Finances are different for soloists, couples, and groups.

Boundaries are important.

Having a legacy, and making an impact, is about more than having kids.

Dying with zero is okay—find a balance of life, money, and health.

Budgeting tells you both what you can and can't spend money on.

It is possible to live a life without debt.

Emergency funds turn a crisis into an inconvenience.

Invest only in things you understand.

Invest toward *your* goals (not other people's goals for you).

Paperwork is important (wills, living wills, POAs).

Insurance provides protection.

Planning ahead for Mom and Dad is easier than responding to an emergency.

To die with zero, you need to bend the net worth curve over time.

You must pay taxes, but you get a choice of when and how.

Buying a house is a choice, not a requirement.

It is okay to spend money on whatever brings you joy.

I don't truly expect you to accept all these mental models. You get to choose the ones that fit you and your life. The key is to be able to identify the difference between your current thinking and alternatives. As you start to plan for your life and finances, realize that your decades of life experience are fighting you. Many of us did not have great examples of money management growing up; don't use that as an excuse not to change. Acknowledge where you came from and be deliberate about where you want to go.

The other challenge for Childfree people is that it can feel like the whole world is against us at times. Our society and culture make up big chunks of the environment that we learn within. It can be a challenge to find a supportive Childfree community. I'm lucky that I have good Childfree friends online who are supportive, but I'm currently living in the Deep South, which is downright hostile to Childfree people. Take the time to realize how your environment and the standard life plan are pushing back against your growth and improving your mental models.

If you want to challenge yourself, take the list of mental models above and rate them. There are some that you probably already do, so mark those as "done." Pick one to three to work on actively and mark them as "doing." And don't be afraid to cross out or mark ones as "dump" if they just don't fit you and your life. Applaud yourself for the ones that you have already done. Work through the ones you are doing, and as you make progress, you can move to other mental models.

As adults, we can only focus on changing one to three things at a time. Keep focus and keep making progress. There will be setbacks. Personally, right now, I'm working on finding balance and embracing FILE in my life, and it is a struggle. I'm just finishing up this book and should take some time to myself, but instead I've got two more books rolling around in my head. I can either beat myself up about not finding a balance, or I can accept my limitations. Same goes for you.

DIVING DEEPER: For more, visit https://childfreewealth.com/4.

COMPATIBLE BAGGAGE

There needs to be a special callout for combining money behaviors as a couple or group. It is hard enough to change your own money behaviors without trying to change with someone else. It is very common for couples to have different money behaviors. I'm amazed by how often there is a clear spender and a clear saver in a couple. Ideally, they rub off on each other to find a balance, but that is not always the case. Interestingly, it is sometimes harder to teach two savers to spend than it is for opposites to come together in the middle.

Couples often need a third party to help them with their financial behaviors. If I had my way, any couple who are getting serious (their judgment of that term) would sit down with a CFP® professional and work through their money behaviors. Consider this the next step up from showing each other your credit reports.

In practice, it is not fair to expect someone else to change their money behaviors for you. They need to change their money behaviors for themselves. Whenever I struggle with this concept, I think back to the concept of "compatible baggage."

Story time. I spent quite a few years in healthcare prior to becoming a CFP®. I was working as a paramedic just before I got married and had a patient encounter that may have changed my entire outlook on life.

My patient had been happily married for forty-two years, so of course I asked him what the secret to being married that long was. Here's what he told me:

"It's not looks, those come and go."

"It's not lust, that comes and goes."

"It's not love, that comes and goes."

At this point I stopped him and reminded him that I was getting married in the next couple of weeks, and he wasn't making me feel so good about it... He continued.

"The secret to a happy marriage is compatible baggage. You both have baggage you bring into the relationship. If you can accept hers and she can accept yours, you will do well. The problem comes when people go into a relationship hoping something will change, as it won't. With compatible baggage you accept the person, good and bad, and if the baggage goes away, your marriage just gets stronger."

Compatible baggage may sound unromantic, but now that we've been married fourteen years, I get it. Both my wife and I are workaholics. If we could not accept that, it would cause strife. My wife doesn't really care about finances and leaves everything to me. At times I'd love her to be more engaged, but I just know that is part of the baggage and I accept it (luckily, she doesn't spend much). We are both committed to being Childfree. For some that would be baggage; for us it is 100% compatible.

With couples, I give them homework to do a compatible baggage assessment. It is a chance to be truly honest with each other. You need to be honest and vulnerable for it to work. If your loved one has baggage that you cannot accept, and they need to change, you need to discuss it now. If they don't want to—or can't—change, then you may have a compatibility issue. The problem is that all too many couples "hint and hope" that their partner will change. It is not fair to expect your other half to be a mind reader.

I've done work with many couples on their finances. Not all of them made it through. There are money behaviors that just don't mix. If one of you is 100% committed to being debt free, and the other one sees nothing wrong with taking out another $50K loan, watch out. On the other hand, if one of you wants to FIRE at fifty, and the other wants to work forever, there is probably a way to work it out. If you both don't like how the other spends money, that is okay as long as it is within the budgeted pocket money. It is all about what is compatible and what is not.

CONCLUSION

What does Childfree Wealth mean to you?

"Childfree Wealth means having the time, money, and freedom to pursue the activities you want. To be able to focus on yourself and your physical, mental, and emotional needs to be healthy and happy."

—FAWN, FORTY-TWO, SINGLE

In the end, living a Childfree life is not better, or worse, than having kids; it is just different. You and your choices are what is going to decide if your life is better or worse than anyone else's, but who is competing anyway?

The key is to first determine the life you want to live, and then make your finances fit. Life is not a static thing, so it is perfectly fine to change both your life and financial goals as you grow and age. Pick up this book each time you have a major life change and recalibrate your plan. You are not following the Standard LifeScript, so it is okay to make changes. There were chapters in this book that may not apply to your current life, but that might help you in the future. Each time you pick it up, you are likely to get something else out of it, and that is intentional.

As a next step, I encourage you to get involved in the Childfree communities online. It is very helpful to have friends and peers who are living a life similar to yours. Not all communities will fit you, and it may be a challenge to find the right one. I started off on the Childfree Reddit, but for me personally I found a better community of Childfree friends on

Facebook. Take a look at communities like the Childfree Convention and Katy's Chasing Creation. Celebrate International Childfree Day on August 1. Collectively, Childfree people represent a large percentage of the population. We all just need to come together and support each other.

ACKNOWLEDGMENTS

This book would not be possible without the help of many. I want to thank the following:

My wife, Vicki.

My Childfree Wealth® Team, including Ashley, Bri, Corrinne, Katy, Kingston, and Rob. You all had a great impact on this book, and I truly appreciate your feedback.

All of my clients who have allowed me to dive into their lives, many of which became frameworks for the principles discussed in this book.

The team at Sourcebooks, most importantly my editor, Erin, and her dog, Cheddar.

A special note of thanks to the Childfree community: Much of this book comes from research I completed in 2022, when I surveyed 299 Childfree people and interviewed 26. Each chapter starts with a quote from one of the surveys or interviews (all anonymized). This book would not be possible without this research and all the Childfree people I have talked to and worked with since then. You will find that while our lives may differ from the "norm" within the Childfree community, there are remarkable similarities. We are all trying to figure out how to live our best life without the Standard LifeScript.

RESOURCES

Advice-Only Planners—https://adviceonlynetwork.com
Aging Life Care Association—https://aginglifecare.org
Chasing Creation—https://chasingcreation.org
Childfree Wealth®—https://childfreewealth.com
Childfree Wealth® Podcast—https://childfreewealth.buzzsprout.com
Freelancers Union—https://freelancersunion.org
IRS Charity List—https://www.irs.gov/charities-non-profits/exempt-organization-types
LLIS—https://llis.com
MakeMyMove—https://makemymove.com
Treasury Direct—https://treasurydirect.com
Trust and Will—https://trustandwill.com
Tutum Journal—https://tutumglobal.com
USPS Informed Delivery—https://www.usps.com/manage/informed-delivery.htm
Undue Medical Debt—https://unduemedicaldebt.org/
Vanguard Charitable—https://www.vanguardcharitable.org

INDEX

M

N

ABOUT THE AUTHOR

Photo credit: John King

Jay Zigmont, PhD, MBA, CFP®, is the founder of Childfree Wealth® (https://childfreewealth.com), a life and financial planning firm dedicated to helping Childfree and Permanently Childless people. Childfree Wealth® is the first life and financial planning firm dedicated to serving Childfree people.

Dr. Jay is a CERTIFIED FINANCIAL PLANNER™, Childfree Wealth Specialist®, and author of the book *Portraits of Childfree Wealth*. Dr. Jay is the co-host of the *Childfree Wealth®* podcast. His PhD is in adult learning from the University of Connecticut.

He has been featured in *Fortune, Forbes,* MarketWatch, *Wall Street Journal, New York Times, Business Insider,* CNBC, and many other publications. In 2023, he was named a Rising Star by Financial Planning.

Made in the USA
Columbia, SC
05 April 2025